This book provides much f
what it means to be church ii
good food it should be digest

*Steve Uppal, preacher, con, ᵣ ....., auṯhor and
senior leader of All Nations Movement*

This clear, insightful and inspiring book paints a strong,
biblically thorough picture of what it means to be the
Church and how we can embrace belonging in it. If you are
asking questions of what the Church really is and if it could
be for you and where you are, this is a must-read.

*Anne Calver, preacher, conference speaker, author of 'Unleashed'
and founder of Unleashed Church*

To cover the Christian journey from personal conversion
and baptism to the universal purpose and significance of the
church is a huge undertaking! Chris is a reassuring guide on
this journey, referring frequently to verses in scripture and
always returning to God's primary nature of love as the core
of all belief, practice and aspiration.

*Jill Baker, preacher, conference speaker, author, former
Vice President of the Methodist Conference (2017-2018),
and former Chair of the Methodist Council (2018-2022)*

In this timely and important work, Chris Horton weaves together a matrix of pivotal relationships that touches on our connection with God, one another and the place and purpose of the Church in the 21st Century. Brilliantly researched and scripturally sound, this book enables us to navigate a course through life's complexities in the knowledge that God has a purpose and destiny for us both as individuals and as a gathered community. I wholeheartedly recommend it.

John Glass, former General Superintendent of the Elim Churches (2000-2016) and former Chair of Council of the Evangelical Alliance (2014-2018)

Belong

Living in God's Family

Chris Horton

ALL NATIONS
PUBLISHING

BELONG: LIVING IN GOD'S FAMILY

Copyright © 2024 Christopher John Horton

Published by All Nations Publishing

ISBN 978-1-7390986-6-7

Cover design by Alisha Bains. www.alishabains.co.uk

Dedicated to all those who, over the years,
have shown me the richness of belonging in God's family

Table of Contents

Introduction

"We are all so much together, but we are all dying of loneliness."

— **Albert Schweitzer**

People feel isolated. Loneliness is perhaps the main characteristic of Western societies and, increasingly, Asian ones too. But God's intention always has been to draw us into relationship with Him and one another, to enjoy the sort of love and family that the Trinity enjoy. So many aspects of modern life cause separation — including religion or trying to reach God through what we do — but Jesus reconciles and brings us together.

When we respond to God's love, we become part of the Body of Christ, the worldwide family, which should be characterised by the same love. We are on a journey and not there yet, but by receiving God's love we can love others and relate with people. It is a process and not always an easy one.

The first section, 'Coming home', looks at the problem of isolation and God's remedy. In the second, 'Living as part of the family', we consider how we can respond and take hold of the remedy for ourselves. When we respond to God, we find He puts us into His family: we are born again into a new household. The implications of this can only be worked out in a local church, rooted together with a handful of people close to us.

The New Testament implies churches will be fruitful when connected relationally to the wider church through apostles and their teams of Ephesians 4:11 ministries, whose role is to enable all Christians to do works of service until we unite. This would seem a vast vision which is beyond our abilities. The third section, 'Among the tribes', attempts to grapple with what the scriptures say about this and what the vision might mean for us in the twenty-first century.

So many Christians act as though they see no need for the church, maybe through the pain that comes when brothers and sisters act or speak in ways that are less than their true identity in Christ. Christians, and therefore churches, are far from perfect yet. But despite its many mistakes and brokenness, Jesus loves His church and died for it. We can choose to follow Him and let Him change us and others to become more like Him or to withdraw into isolation.

These short chapters are an attempt to share my love for God and His people in a way that will encourage readers to live as part of a Christ-centred community. You may need grace to persevere in living like this, or to find or return to such a community, or to pioneer a new one together with others who want to gather around Jesus. Whichever is true for you, God's invitation is to "come home."

Coming home

1. Belong? Not me!

Deep within each of us is a longing to belong. We need to be loved and to find a place or some context where we can be ourselves and call home. We might mean different things by 'home' and have varying hopes and dreams for belonging. But all human beings share this deep desire to belong. It is part of being human.

What sort of image comes to mind when you think of home? I think of warmth. My childhood was in a warm environment in at least two senses — my dad discovered the joys of central heating after growing up in a draughty and cold house, so he loved to turn up the thermostat in the evening. It was also a warm and loving place where my sister and I knew we always belonged. Whatever might happen at school or elsewhere, home was where every trauma could be sorted, each misunderstanding could be explained, new adventures could be planned and questions would always be answered. We did not have to try to belong, we just did.

However, we all have mixed experiences of home life. Even in the most loving of homes, parents and siblings make mistakes. We all carry some wounds, or some brokenness, even if we have mostly enjoyed a loving home. We all say and do things that are less than loving and kind. And there is worse. Many recall the pain of hearing parents rowing, the loss and abandonment of a parent leaving. Some people can recall only the pain of abuse and alienation at home. For them, home was not a positive experience or a safe place from which to explore the world. Home can be more like hell than heaven — a place to escape from rather than a place to belong. But every one of us has some mix of the two in our background.

The Bible explains that when God first made the world, it was good and perfect (Genesis 1). God said of everything that it was "good" (except when He made man, when "good" came only after He had also made woman: Genesis 2). People were able to enjoy friendship with God; that was His intention for humankind from the start and it is a beautiful picture of friendship that Adam and Eve could walk in the Garden of Eden with Him.

But that changed radically through the Fall (Genesis 3). The Bible does not try to paint a rosy picture of what has happened to make the world such a place of paradox, where heavenly landscapes and loving relationships are mixed with hell-like earthquakes or broken relationships. We have to face the fact that, whatever the precise detail of what happened in Genesis 3, human beings have acted independently from God and it has caused angst and alienation. We are aliens to God and He to us, yet because we were made to enjoy friendship with Him, it is painful and people find all sorts of ways of masking the pain and frustration of being separated from God. Some obvious examples of covering the pain are drugs or alcohol, but there are others that are perhaps less obvious, like over-work or religious activities. At best, they cover the problem for a while, but the root is separation or alienation.

Humankind became alienated from God and lost friendship with Him as a result. We have also been alienated from ourselves, from others and from the rest of creation, and we will touch on each of these in the next four chapters. But there is good news to come as we do so: Jesus said, "I came that they may have life and have it abundantly" (John 10:10). He also explained that this life was eternal but starting now. And what is eternal life? "This is eternal life," Jesus said, "that they may know you, the only true God, and Jesus Christ whom you have sent" (John 17:3). Eternal life is knowing Him, friendship restored.

2. Distanced

We feel alienated — at a distance from God — and instinctively many people want to try to bridge the gap somehow. That is religion: trying to get to God. It seems like such a good thing but it does not work. It is human effort, whether in the form of prayers, chants or songs, rituals or sacrifices, ethical decisions or using drugs of various kinds to change how we feel about the world. If God really is there, a perfect Person, the supreme Being and holy, then human efforts will never be enough to reach Him.

Instead, the good news about Jesus is that He is God coming to us. He has made it possible to bridge the gap. But to understand how, we need to establish what has caused the separation.

People of every culture, with whatever worldview, philosophy or religious belief, know what it is to do wrong or 'sin.' Some might think of sin more as behaving in a shameful way that brings dishonour to the family or community. Some might think of sin as failing to conform to expected standards of behaviour or acting as though outside the community. Others, particularly in the West, usually think of sin as stepping over a line that should not be crossed or disobeying a law or command.

Whatever the worldview and however sin might be understood, everyone knows what it is like to cause offence and to feel guilt or shame. The scriptures teach that sin makes a barrier, and Isaiah 59:2 is just one of many places we can see this: "Your iniquities have been barriers between you and your God, and your sins have hidden his face from you."

Christian theologians have different views on whether sin is inherent in being human (so that we are born with a tendency to sin because of an 'original sin') or that sin is so prevalent around us that we quickly learn to do so. As a parent and grandparent, I have observed that a very young child does not need much teaching to be self-centred. Even before speaking, they can exert their independent will in a way that disregards others. As children grow, they usually become more self-aware, more conscious of the effect their behaviour has on others. But sadly, they cross the line. We all do. What is more, God knows we sin. It causes Him pain when we choose to live independently of Him.

As so often, we need to look at the first book of the Bible to understand this concept. Genesis 3 paints a dramatic and poetic picture of the first sinful choices. Whether we are reading about a literal one man and one woman or a symbolic story, the message is the same. Much of the language in Genesis is symbolic, and to me that suggests this is an idealised narrative that expresses the truth of what happened in symbols or types. However we interpret it, the important thing is we believe this is truth and has meaning for us. The command was clear: "Do not eat that fruit!" The temptation to disobey that command was not a direct "Just do it!" Instead, it came in a subtle way through questioning what God said and why. That started Eve and then Adam thinking as though they could live independently from God. They were, in effect, setting themselves up as being His equals, able to decide whether or not He was correct.

The essence of sin is to live independently of God. We were designed and created to live as a community dependent on Him and in union with Him. Adam and Eve had the potential to become mature through living or 'abiding' in Him. However, they chose otherwise, and the consequences were far more serious than expected: death came into the creation for the first time. Our experience as humans is that we do wrong and feel guilty as a result, even if we try to cover it up by keeping busy or deadening the senses. Underneath, we know something is not right. We have an inborn longing for peace and connection but cannot experience it until we repent and receive His forgiveness.

We must repent and trust, or rely, on Jesus to benefit from the good news. If the essence of sin is independence, the essence of being free from sin and its consequences is to depend and rely on Jesus. We will think about repentance in Chapter 9 and other aspects of depending on Him in Chapters 10 to 13. But for now let's focus on what enables us to benefit. The technical term is 'atonement', which includes reconciliation and what is needed to make good what was wrong. The good news is that Jesus sacrificed Himself to atone for our sins.

What happened at the Cross is described in various ways in scripture. These address different ways of understanding sin, some making more sense in certain cultures. However, the main reason that there are several different words, concepts, images or symbols to describe it is that we are trying to understand with human minds a mystery that has spiritual as well as human and historical aspects. The events of the crucifixion and resurrection of Jesus were historical and there is good evidence for the supernatural miracle of resurrection. But it is hard to explain God giving Himself up to death at the hands of humans and even more challenging when we realise there is only one God but three Persons. If we make too much separation between Father, Son and Spirit, we end up thinking of three gods. Yet if we do not consider the separate Persons, we have the impossible situation of the One who upholds creation dying, so the world should have ended abruptly.

There are several ways the New Testament describes atonement: ransom, redemption, healing, eternal life, new covenant, sacrifice, substitution, victory, the revelation of God's love, reconciliation, and exchange. (There is a mix of metaphors and descriptions, and I have tried to explain them all briefly in the Appendix.) Each one sheds light on the key event in history: the crucifixion and resurrection of Jesus. They all have an element of the truth, but some are more significant than others in the New Testament. Above all, we must view atonement not in a dispassionate, academic way but through a relationship with Jesus. At the end of the day, what matters is to encounter Jesus, acknowledge Him as Lord and receive.

3. Confused

The story of Cain and Abel in Genesis 4 is a simple one but not entirely easy to understand. Both offer a sacrifice to God out of the work they do. Cain tills the ground and brings some of its fruit, while Abel tends livestock and gives some of the firstlings. Why does God accept Abel's offering but not Cain's? Scripture is not clear, but perhaps it is to do with effort. Cain labours to work the ground, while Abel relies on God's provision more directly. Maybe there is an indication of the danger of being religious, trying to please God when God has already made available all that is necessary for us.

Whatever the reason, and however they realised it, Cain now had a problem. He was disappointed and envious of his brother. Even this was not a sin. God said if Cain did not do well, then sin was crouching at the door, wanting to master him, but he must master it. It is not inevitable that we should do something sinful. Sin is a powerful force but we have a choice whether to give in to it or not. Over time, if we keep making wrong choices, it gets harder to refuse sin. That is why Paul refers to sin as a bad husband in Romans 7, in that we can only be free from it through death (being identified with Jesus in His death and included 'in Christ').

Cain gives in to sin, though. He entices his brother into a field and kills him. Whether people choose to interpret Cain and Abel as symbolic figures or literally two individuals, what matters is how they illustrate the problem of sin. Not only is Cain distanced from God but he is alienated from his family as God's judgement was that he should be separated from them. Perhaps this was to stop them from taking revenge on him or maybe the inevitable consequence of sin is that we are alienated from those around us.

Cain was condemned to settle in the land of Nod, which means "no settlement." He wanted a place to live and raise a family. As soon as his wife bore a son, he built a city and named it after him. Like all humans, he wanted his life to be significant and to have a permanent memorial, but he tried to achieve this through his own efforts rather than relying on God. It is a pattern repeated in every generation and by each of us. We try to achieve something through our efforts. We try to create something permanent. We want to be secure and at peace, so we try accumulating possessions and wealth. We want to escape the confusion and the difficulties of settling in a place called "no settlement." These are deep desires in every human heart. However, no matter how hard we try, it just does not work.

The Tower of Babel in Genesis 11 is another example of this attempt to create something worthwhile and permanent. It is implied that the tower was a way of reaching God. But the Lord "came down" to view it. Every attempt to reach God or achieve a permanent and significant memorial will fail. When we rely on God and trust Him, allowing Him to be Lord and direct us, and give up our independence, that is when we find He has done all that is necessary to bridge the gap between Him and us.

There is a way of escaping the confusion and finding peace and meaning in our lives. But it demands that we rely on God and depend on what He has done rather than what we can do.

4. Strangers

Researchers are discovering what human beings have instinctively known since the beginning of time: people need people. There is a deep yearning for community in each of us.

An academic psychologist, Matthew Lieberman, reported on a survey of people's social connections that was carried out in 1985 and again in 2004.[1] The researchers asked, "Over the last six months, who are the people with whom you discussed matters important to you?" In 1985, the most common number was three (59% of respondents listed three people). But in 2004, the most common number was zero — none. Over 25% had no one, compared with 10% in 1985. And only 37% of respondents in 2004 could list three or more friends. Matthew Lieberman writes, "One out of every four of us is walking around with no one to share our lives with." The title of his book suggests that this is an unnatural state of affairs as we are designed for more and better.

Not only do we long for social and emotional connections with other people, but our health is affected. In another academic study, researchers found that real social

---

[1] See Lieberman *Social: Why Our Brains Are Wired to Connect*

interactions reduce the risk of mental illness.[2] "Frequency of in-person social contact with friends and family," they reported in 2015, "independently predicts risk of subsequent depression in older adults. Clinicians should consider encouraging face-to-face social interactions as a preventive strategy for depression."

As we read the Bible, we should not be surprised by this. The story of Cain and Abel shows not only that sin causes confusion or lack of peace in the sinner but also that it breaks connections with other people. Abel is dead. His parents are devastated and no doubt face the pain of losing two sons, one as a victim of murder and one as a victim of his own sin. This tragic turn of events was not how God had intended it to be. In creation, He made men and women in His image, in the image of the one God in three Persons. God Himself is both one and a community characterised by self-giving love.

Living estranged from one another was not how God intended humans to live, yet the infinite God, who is outside time, saw that this would happen. He saw from the start the need for a way out of the problem. That is why Jesus is "destined before the foundation of the world" (1 Peter 1:20)

---

[2] See Teo et al "Does Mode of Contact with Different Types of Social Relationships Predict Depression in Older Adults? Evidence from a Nationally Representative Survey"

even though not revealed until the end of the old age and the beginning of the new creation. In the same way, God is outside time, so Jesus is "eternally begotten" even though He was born as a human at a point in time 2,000 years ago.

God's plan was for humans to be a loving community in the image of the Triune God, whose nature is love. Sin causes us to be alienated from one another, but throughout the Old Testament, God draws people together as prophetic signs of the new creation and the new community He is forming. It begins with Abraham's family (significantly, this is straight after the Tower of Babel incident). The family becomes a clan and then a whole people by the time of Moses.

Later, something interesting happens. The people of God do not increase but decrease. Some tribes lose their distinctive identity as worshippers of God earlier than others. Under King David, there is a renewal, and the people quickly grow in influence as a direct result of their devotion to God and unity. Yet this is lost rapidly as King Solomon's heart strays, and the nation splits in two after his death. The northern tribes quickly descend into idolatry, followed soon after by Judah and Benjamin. Still, the prophets, who are a minority in all the tribes, call the people back to their identity as a community that worships and reflects the character of the one true God.

During His earthly ministry, when Jesus was living and working in Palestine 2,000 years ago, He speaks of Himself as the Son of Man. This identifies Him as the Messianic King whom Daniel saw in a vision (Daniel 7). It identifies Him as human and is one of the indications that the people of God have been reduced to just one man: at this time, God's Chosen People consist solely of Jesus. This is no accident. Jesus deliberately and carefully teaches that He will begin a new creation and expand the Chosen People to be defined not by genetics and genealogy, like the existing creation, but by the Spirit and new birth. The people of God who inherit the promises made to Abraham back at the beginning of this process are now defined by being 'in Christ'. Paul explains this in Galatians 3:27–29:

> As many of you as were baptized into Christ have clothed yourselves with Christ. There is no longer Jew or Greek, there is no longer slave or free, there is no longer male and female; for all of you are one in Christ Jesus. And if you belong to Christ, then you are Abraham's offspring, heirs according to the promise.

This new people, the forerunners of a new creation, came into existence on the day of Pentecost when the Spirit filled the disciples as they were together (Acts 2). They were devoting themselves to prayer and encouraging one another.

No doubt they were trying to make sense of what had happened and to understand what Jesus meant in the various things He said. Suddenly, the Spirit came upon them in a dramatic fashion and transformed them.

No longer confused, they were ready to demonstrate and explain the supernatural presence of God. No longer fearful, they could proclaim the truth. Peter boldly reminded the crowd that they had crucified Jesus just a few weeks before, and now He was raised and ascended as the Lord of all. No longer squabbling and competitive, now they were formed into a new community characterised by love. No wonder many in the crowd were convinced and wanted to follow Jesus.

Of course, ever since, we have been living in the overlap between the old creation and the new, the "present evil age" (Galatians 1:4) and the "age to come" (Mark 10:30 and Ephesians 2:7). We still make mistakes. There are examples in the New Testament and church history of greed, selfishness and bitter disagreements. But the new creation has begun and the invitation to become part of the people of God extends to all who are willing to acknowledge Jesus as Lord, to surrender independence and rely totally on Him, and to be incorporated into His Body.

The big issue in New Testament times was the division between Jews and Gentiles. According to Jewish tradition, everyone who was not born Jewish or willing to become a proselyte was outside the people of God, and for many years Christians from Gentile backgrounds were regarded as inferior by most Jewish followers of Jesus. Paul, however, had an even bigger vision from God of just how radical the new creation is. In many of his letters, he explains that Jews and Gentiles are one in Christ and pleads for love, unity and honour towards one another. Ephesians 2:11–22 is an extended passage that teaches this clearly. God has actually now abolished the Jewish Law "so that he might create in himself one new humanity in place of the two, thus making peace…. Through him [Jesus] both of us have access in one Spirit to the Father." Paul can assure the Gentiles, "You are no longer strangers and aliens, but you are citizens with the saints and also members of the household of God, built upon the foundation of the apostles and prophets, with Christ Jesus himself as the cornerstone."

A new creation has started. A new community has been formed. We are no longer alienated from each other if we are in Christ and part of His Body. That is really good news.

5. Thorns and earthquakes

Cutting through brambles overgrowing a path or trying to uproot them in the garden, I often remember the curse Adam brought on himself. God pronounced judgement because Adam disobeyed:

> "...cursed is the ground because of you;
> in toil you shall eat of it all the days of your life;
> thorns and thistles it shall bring forth for you;
> and you shall eat the plants of the field.
> By the sweat of your face
> you shall eat bread..." (Genesis 3:17b–19a)

In other words, everything is hard work instead of the original fruitfulness that flows effortlessly from relying on God's grace.

Digging up brambles usually involves some scratches and, quite often, thorns being embedded in my skin. But that is a very minor problem compared to the major issues of natural disasters and now global warming. Earthquakes, volcanoes, tornadoes, tidal waves, forest fires and extreme storms have plagued the earth throughout history. Does God intend the disasters that keep happening? In a word, no! God wants all people to be saved, and that includes being kept safe (1 Timothy 2:4). But He allows the consequences of sinful behaviour in a fallen world to affect people as a warning.

God is all-powerful. Therefore, many people argue that He cannot be loving if disasters happen. This view is too simplistic and imagines that God is limited to being like a human. There is a mystery — we cannot understand God fully — but we know God is loving. It is His nature (1 John 4:7–11). Because of His love, He created humans in His image, with the power to choose between friendship with Him or rebellion against Him. He does not force anyone to make a decision. He loves us and desires a response of love from humankind but allows us to make our own responses.

So many responses by humans over history have been rebellious. There are many things wrong with the world as a result. Humans are out of relationship with God, each other and the rest of creation. God allows the consequences of our wrong choices to flow (Psalm 81:11–12). But we can receive these consequences as a warning or reminder to us all to turn to God.

It is too simplistic to say that bad things only happen to bad people; that is clearly not the case. In fact, there are consequences of sin and greed that affect everyone. Even earthquakes or other natural disasters, as well as plagues, are indirectly the result of humankind's mismanagement of creation. The earth is not functioning as God originally intended.

The whole of creation is subject to decay (or "futility," as stated in Romans 8:20) and is longing for God's people, the church, to fulfil the calling God gave to humankind in the very beginning (Romans 8:18–25). So Christians, of all people, should not moan about the difficulties of living in a fallen world. Our purpose is, instead, to demonstrate what life is like when we love God in response to His love and overflow with God's love towards other people. When the children of God behave like His children and respond to Him in obedience, Paul teaches, even the troubled creation will be healed.

There are beautiful images of this future healing in Revelation 21 and 22, which describes the new (or renewed) heaven and earth. The essential characteristic is God's presence: "God's dwelling place is now among the people, and he will dwell with them. They will be his people, and God himself will be with them and be their God" (Revelation 21:3). Death is no more. The heavenly city has come down to earth and is beautiful and complete. Heaven and earth are united — the natural and the supernatural in complete harmony. The river of life flows from God's throne and "on either side of the river is the tree of life with its twelve kinds of fruit, producing its fruit each month; and the leaves of the tree are for the healing of nations" (Revelation 22:2).

God's presence. Wholeness. Fruit. Life. Healing. What a picture of the reversal that the Cross has made possible! "Through him [Jesus] God was pleased to reconcile to himself all things, whether on earth or in heaven, by making peace through the blood of his cross" (Colossians 1:20). The fruit of the tree in the Garden of Eden was taken in rebellion but the fruit of the tree of life is freely available because of the reconciliation Jesus has achieved. There are 12 kinds of fruit, showing God's abundant provision for all people, symbolised by the 12 tribes. All people groups will receive healing and the creation will be completely restored.

Meanwhile, we live in the old, tired creation that is wrecked and distorted by sin and its consequences. We cannot fully understand how the results of any individual's sin or the whole sinfulness of mankind result in specific events. Still, we know they are the consequence of judgement, a curse that humanity has brought upon itself. But we also live with hope that the new creation has begun (2 Corinthians 5:17). We see signs of it and pray "Your Kingdom come" until He brings all natural and spiritual forces under His control. Jesus could command the waves to quieten down, and they did. He gives us the same right to pray and speak peace. The Kingdom is here among us, but it is also coming and not yet fully revealed. Theologians call this 'inaugurated eschatology' or 'partially realised eschatology.'[3] The things promised at the end exist in part here because Jesus' death and resurrection changed everything, but they will only fully be here when He returns at the end of time. Sometimes we see miraculous answers to prayer and sometimes we do not, but we still have the miraculous presence of God with us in the pain and difficulty.

Brambles are tiny compared with the earthquakes, deforestation and drought that we see worldwide. But every time I get scratched, it is a reminder to pray for the significant issues facing the creation as a result of human sinfulness. We are alienated from the natural world, but "Your Kingdom come!"

---

[3] **Eschatology is the study of the 'last things' or the end of the age, so these two phrases mean that the things to do with the end of the age have already begun.**

6. God at home with Himself?

Many people say they believe in God, even in the contemporary Western cultures. Of course, this masks a great variety of views and is only a record of what people believe or think intellectually: the proportion of people who make decisions about how to live based on their relationship with God is much smaller.

What kind of God or supreme being do we imagine? For most people, God is a distant force, maybe a prime mover who set up the world like a clockmaker and then stepped back to watch it wind down. For many, God is pictured as a bearded grandfather: nice but not very strong and living at a distance. For many, God is a divine force at work in creation and perhaps sensed by connecting with spirit beings.

How does the Bible reveal God? We can sum up the revelation of scripture in two words: holy Father. He is holy — perfect and different from us in kind. Jesus speaks of God as being spirit (John 4:24). So, He is invisible to human eyes and does not have a human body. He is infinite and present everywhere at once. He is beyond understanding.

He is holy, but He is also Father, separate from us but also close. There are many references in the Old Testament to this, but again it is Jesus who reveals it most clearly by talking to and about His *Abba*, a Hebrew word that conveys both intimacy ("Daddy") and respect. I am very conscious as a father that no human father is perfect. We are all aware that there are many people for whom the word itself brings up memories of abuse and produces a reaction of pain, perhaps mixed with revulsion, fear, hatred and many other negative emotions. God, however, is the perfect Father, the only one who always acts entirely out of love.

Jesus is also God, "the exact imprint of God's very being," (Hebrews 1:3), in other words the image of the invisible God. The Greek word for "imprint" implies it is like a coin produced in a mould, bearing the exact likeness of the ruler who commissioned the coin. We know quite a lot about Jesus' time on earth from the New Testament, but the Bible also reveals Him as always existing outside time: "In the beginning was the Word," John writes, "and the Word was with God and the Word was God" (John 1:1).

The Spirit is also God. Because the Spirit is spirit and therefore not sensed by human means, it is hard for us to picture what the Spirit is like. One scholar explains, "…we begin to know the Spirit when we begin to realise that our ability to recognise and respond to Christ and His Father does not have its source in us but is given to us from outside ourselves. The Holy Spirit stands with us on our side of the encounter with the Father and Son and makes it possible for us to know and confess them."[4]

It took a lot of prayerful study, debate and some strong disagreements for the church to arrive at an understanding of the Trinity because it is so hard to picture one God existing in three Persons. It does not make sense to human minds. The arithmetic does not add up. But this understanding is vital as we experience God, follow Him and come to know God better.

It matters because if Jesus is not God, then His death on the Cross is not sufficient for our salvation. As God, He demonstrated God's self-sacrificing love and made possible the exchange of our sinfulness for His righteousness. It matters because if the Spirit is not God but just some spiritual force, then we cannot truly experience friendship with God or His presence with us. It matters above all because if God is alone before creation, then love cannot be His main characteristic, and something is missing in God until He made people to love. Instead, He always was and is and will be complete and a loving community of three Persons.

God is at home in Himself in Trinity. If we place too much emphasis on God as one, there is a danger of solitariness

---

[4] See Smail *The Giving Gift: Holy Spirit in Person* p. 30

being the definition of creation when it actually demonstrates community and fruitfulness. If we place too much emphasis on God as three Persons, we are in danger of seeing three gods, not one. We have to embrace both extremes — one God and three Persons — to avoid the problem of confusion and reducing God to human terms. In the same way, we must embrace both extremes of God being holy (distant because completely perfect and separate from us) and being the perfect Father (intimate and very close to us). A muddled compromise does not do justice to the revelation of God in scripture. Instead, there comes a point where words are inadequate and we should no longer try to understand but kneel in worship.

7. The God who left home to bring us home

It was an amazing privilege to become a parent: Catherine and I have been blessed with three children and now five grandchildren. When we related with our children and grandchildren as babies, we delighted in watching them learn and adapt in response to various sounds and other experiences. We humans see the world through our experiences, and our understanding of the world begins with ourselves. As we grow up, our understanding develops into a worldview which we largely inherit from what our parents and others say. It is a corporate experience built up over generations.

But as Christians, our understanding of the world and existence originates much further back, right at the very start. The first words of the Bible are "In the beginning, God…" (Genesis 1:1). We do not start with our self-understanding, nor even with trying to piece together some logic from the things we experience, even though that is how every baby begins to understand the world and to communicate. We start with the beginning: God Himself. What is He like? One word can sum up so much: love.

We have considered the problem: we are alienated from God, ourselves, others and the creation. We are alone and yet have a deep longing to be at home. God's remedy is not to whisk us away to some other place called "home" but to move into the creation and make a home among us. We cannot reach Him — He is spirit and beyond us — but God extends a warm welcome to us because He is the very definition of love. We can picture salvation as God inviting us to sit by a warm fireside with Him.

God takes the initiative because of love. Any religious efforts to try to please Him as a way of getting home or being accepted in His family are totally ineffective. God came to us in the form of a man, Jesus, and since His resurrection and ascension to heaven, He now comes to us by the Spirit.

Many theologians have struggled to explain how a loving and all-powerful God can allow suffering. The theme has already come up several times in this book. Perhaps the most helpful way to approach the question is to focus on how God comes among us, above all in the Incarnation, God becoming a human being in Jesus, with all the limitations that involved. His humanity was absolute, so even in the miracles He performed, He limited Himself to what humans can do when filled with the Holy Spirit. But Jesus went far beyond these limitations: He humbled Himself and entered fully into human suffering.

In the aftermath of the Second World War, struggling to make sense of the horrors and the guilt felt by many, the German theologian Jürgen Moltmann wrote about

"The Crucified God" as the foundation of Christian faith and theology. God is not just an impartial observer from a distance but is intimately involved in human suffering. Moltmann wrote:

> When God becomes man in Jesus of Nazareth, he not only enters into the finitude of man, but in his death on the cross also enters into the situation of man's godforsakenness. In Jesus he does not die the natural death of a finite being, but the violent death of the criminal on the cross, the death of complete abandonment by God. The suffering in the passion of Jesus is abandonment, rejection by God, his Father. God does not become a religion, so that man participates in him by corresponding religious thoughts and feelings. God does not become a law, so that man participates in him through obedience to a law. God does not become an ideal, so that man achieves community with him through constant striving. He humbles himself and takes upon himself the eternal death of the godless and the godforsaken, so that all the godless and the godforsaken can experience communion with him.[5]

[5] See Moltmann *The Crucified God: The Cross of Christ as the Foundation and Criticism of Christian Theology* p. 276

Jesus came to suffer and to save us from suffering. In the Appendix, we look at some of the ways the Bible describes what happened when Jesus died and rose again. These descriptions help us understand something of the atonement and how it enables us to reconcile with God. We are saved from sin and from the consequences of sin. We are set free from death and share in Jesus' victory. But what does it mean to be saved? Is it mainly about going to heaven, and if so, what does that mean? Let's look at this in the next chapter.

8. A heavenly home

Many think of salvation as going to heaven when they die. This may be because religious paintings and Greek philosophy have given many Christians the idea that heaven is a place, a spiritual place but separate in geography and time from where we are on earth. It is easy to assume heaven is a future place or state. However, the Bible paints many pictures of heaven as a spiritual dimension that is closely connected to the earth, so close that the natural and the supernatural affect each other directly. Heaven is primarily God's dwelling place. Our hope for the future is not so much that we shall be whisked away from a terrible earth to a beautiful heaven but that God's dwelling place will encompass new heavens and a new earth united together.[6]

John's Gospel uses the phrase "eternal life" repeatedly, giving another perspective on what it means for the Kingdom of God to come (the other Gospels frequently refer to the Kingdom). In John 17:3, Jesus defines what He means: "And this is eternal life, that they may know You, the only true God, and Jesus Christ whom you have sent." Of course, Jesus speaks of other aspects of eternal life: it flows from

---

[6] See Chapter 6. Paula Gooder has written a very helpful book exploring what the scriptures say about heaven, appropriately called *Heaven*.

within and is like living water bubbling up (John 7:37–39). But the essence of eternal life is to *know* Him, to be His friends. And it does not start at some time in the future but now, because "in Him was life" (John 1:4).

Paul picks up the same idea too, often teaching about us being "in Christ." For example, in Colossians 3:3, he says, "for you have died, and your life is hidden with Christ in God." Back in John's Gospel, we pick up the image of God's home with many lovely places for us to live: "In my Father's house there are many dwelling places. If it were not so, would I have told you that I go to prepare a place for you? And if I go and prepare a place for you, I will come again and will take you to myself, that where I am, there you may be also" (John 14:2–3). It is a lovely picture of coming home. It could be seen as a future home "in heaven" until we read on the next few verses.

Jesus says, "And you know the way to the place where I am going." Thomas replies by asking the critical question the rest of the disciples probably wanted to ask: "Lord, we don't know where you are going, so how can we know the way?" (John 14:4–5). If Peter is the impulsive leader among the Twelve, who jumps in and commits himself without thinking, Thomas is the reflective thinker who wants to understand so he can devote himself fully. Jesus' reply is transformational: "I am the way." We do not get to see the route on a map, nor are we given a signpost. Instead, we are invited into a friendship with the Person who will lead us step by step as we develop that friendship. And when we do so, we realise that heaven is eternal life starting now and perfectly fulfilled later when Jesus returns.

Heaven is not a place as we understand places. And it is not populated by spirit beings that are wisps or shadows, like the shades of Greek myths. Instead, the spiritual dimension gives meaning and purpose to the human, physical dimensions. It is more real than human flesh and blood and the physical universe, not less.

There is a wonderful illustration of heaven in C. S. Lewis' story for children of all ages, *The Last Battle*. At the end of the book, the characters find themselves in a delightful place that is like the countries they knew, but better. One explains, "When Aslan said you could never go back to Narnia, he meant the Narnia you were thinking of. But that was not the real Narnia. That had a beginning and an end. It was only a shadow or copy of the real Narnia which has always been here and always will be here: just as our world, England and all, is only a shadow or copy of something in Aslan's real world."[7]

---

[7] See Lewis *The Last Battle* p. 159

Another character responds a little later, "I have come home at last! This is my real country. I belong here. This is the land I have been looking for all my life, though I never knew it till now. The reason why we loved the old Narnia is that it sometimes looked a little like this!"[8]

When we see what God is like and how much He loves us, when we glimpse the heavenly home available to us, the eternal life that consists of knowing Him, we instinctively want to respond.

Our experiences, including some unhelpful ones, train our reactions and responses — so we might feel obligated to do the right thing or to justify His love to some extent by responding well. Sometimes even being thankful is a subconscious way of earning that love. God, however, wants us to respond freely and wholeheartedly. And we can. Thankfulness is a part of it, but in Acts 2:38, Peter clearly stated the foundational responses that lead to being at home, securely part of the family of God. We will explore these in the next section.

---

[8] **See Lewis *The Last Battle* p. 160**

Living as part of the family

9. What must I do? Repent

The dramatic events of Pentecost are recounted in Acts 2. The Holy Spirit came in a very tangible and down-to-earth way, bringing not just a sense of God's presence into a worship and prayer meeting but power that caused the apostles to overflow with thankfulness in the centre of the city where Jesus had been crucified just weeks earlier. Jerusalem was the base of the religious and political establishment that had handed Him over to the Romans.

Now the force of the disciples' experience of the Spirit meant they were very much in public and no longer afraid of suffering consequences. It is as though the Spirit wanted to demonstrate right from the start that this event was fulfilling the promise in Acts 1:8, "But you will receive power when the Holy Spirit has come on you; and you shall be my witnesses..."

Theologians often refer to the coming of the Spirit as the birth of the church. This is an important truth. The presence of God is what makes a church a church. From now on, the people of God would be defined not as those who keep the Law but those who are filled with the Spirit. Paul teaches this clearly in Galatians 3 (especially verses 2 and 5) and it is implied or expressed in many of his other letters. Even the Jewish feast of Pentecost gives an indication of this: it was the celebration of the beginning of harvest and by New Testament times had become associated with the giving of the Law, which is what defined the Old Testament people of God. Now even the feast of Pentecost was fulfilled. There was a harvest of lives being saved and the New Testament people of God came into existence.

However, it is also important to see that the church does not exist for its own benefit, and not even just to praise God in worship and prayer meetings. The church exists to be God's instrument in bringing in the Kingdom, to demonstrate the wisdom and character of God to the spiritual and human 'powers that be' (Ephesians 3:10) and to fulfil the Great Commission.

So the disciples are soon out on the streets. They are quickly noticed, and people have different reactions as they try to understand what is going on. It is time for Peter to explain what is happening and he stands with the rest of the Eleven (no longer an individualist leading on his own) to proclaim the truth. This is a glorious contrast with the nervous follower of Jesus trying to hide in the dark on the night Jesus was betrayed. He does not pull his punches. Peter proclaims that Jesus, whom "you crucified and killed by the hands of those outside the Law" (Acts 2:23) is the long-awaited Messiah, raised from the dead and now exalted in the heavenly places with the Father.

This is preaching the Kingdom, bringing a challenge to submit to King Jesus, not easing people in gently but demanding allegiance to Him. It is the first evangelistic preaching in history, and the activity of the Holy Spirit in the hearts of those hearing causes many to respond. Only the Spirit can convince people that they need to change (John 16:8–11). Our words, when inspired by the Spirit, are the vehicle, but God's Spirit does the work in a human's heart, which is the spiritual aspect of their being.

"What must we do to be saved?" is the cry of a tender conscience throughout history. The question could easily be "How can I know God?" or "How can I find peace and my real home?" The answer is perhaps surprising. Not "Believe that Jesus died for you," (at least, not if by "believe" we mean merely to agree it is true). Nor "Come to Him and He will give you…" The answer is "Repent and be baptised, each of you" (Acts 2:38).

Repent. It is a strange word and may often be misunderstood. "Repent, for the kingdom of heaven has come near" was the basic message John the Baptist brought (Matthew 3:2) and Jesus proclaimed the same message

(Matthew 4:17). It is the first response to God being King or Lord. He demands absolute allegiance above anyone or anything else. And that means change because we are naturally focused on our own needs and wants.

Many people assume repentance means feeling sorry for what we have done wrong. That is a part of it but not the whole story. Repent, in fact, means a change of thinking and of reacting to the circumstances of life. The Greek word used is literally a change of mind, but that does not imply it is enough to change a theory and adopt a new one. The kind of change of mind Jesus demands, and we see modelled in the New Testament, is a complete transformation of life, demonstrated in very practical actions. When Zacchaeus repented, he changed from being a self-centred cheat to a generous giver (Luke 19:1–10). When the Philippian jailer repented, he changed from being a harsh torturer to a servant who would bathe his prisoners' wounds (Acts 16:16–34). It seems God knows our hearts and touches the things that we hold dear or that have become part of our identity, so that repentance might mean surrendering to Him and turning away from different things for each of us.

Repentance is a reversal. Perhaps the best way to think of it is to walk in one direction and then turn around and walk in exactly the opposite direction. That is how radical a change it is when we truly repent. When I repented, I stopped following my independent choices (going the way I chose to go) and instead started going the way Jesus directed me.

When we repent, our lives become totally transformed. There are many testimonies of people who were addicted to various things, being completely changed and freed at the moment they repented. But transformation is a process and does not occur totally in a moment, however dramatic our encounter with God might be and however much freedom there is from drink, drugs, pornography or whatever. Over weeks, months and years, we become more like Jesus as we are led by the Spirit, and we will think about this more in later chapters.

I was fortunate not to have invited into my life any controlling addictions or other dramatic sins before I became a Jesus-follower. So, repentance was not such an obvious change of behaviour for me. But I can remember realising how my lifestyle and the way I spoke to people were very self-centred. Everything seemed to revolve around what I wanted, so I had to repent of that just as wholeheartedly and sincerely as anyone with a more dramatic testimony.

Many people, especially those brought up in a Christian home, can fail to see just how sinful they can be while still seeming to be "nice Christians" on the outside. We might think we are not proud or judgemental until we notice that we are always criticising people for being less spiritual or for some particular sin. We might not think we are selfish and uncaring until we notice how painful it is to give away a treasured possession when the Spirit prompts us to.

Worst of all, we might not realise we are detached from God, not abiding in Jesus or led by the Spirit, when we are using mere human understanding or knowledge. We can even justify this by the truth that there is good wisdom in many other contexts.

It is true that even the most ungodly people are still made in the image of God and part of His creation, capable of exploring the world and bringing helpful insights. There is nothing wrong with human skill or wisdom if we use it in co-operation with God and allow the Spirit to lead us in all our decisions and behaviour. But there is everything wrong with trying to live independently from God and allowing human wisdom to dictate what we do. Paul calls this living from the flesh, in contrast to living in the Spirit (Romans 8). The words and actions might be the same, but the motivation and the presence of God through the Spirit makes all the difference.

The remedy for all these continuing sinful attitudes is the same. First, repent. Then allow the Spirit to change us, as we shall think about in later chapters. Repentance is usually our last resort, but it is God's starting point: when we give Jesus control of our lives, we find true freedom, because only then can He change us and lead us.

10. What must I do? Baptism

It was in August 1976 that I was baptised, at a Christian youth camp where I was one of the leaders. I was seventeen years old and had been a Christian for several years, so I thought I knew everything. As the evening talks led the young people through the salvation story to the point of response, the speaker was clear that baptism was part of the foundation of the Christian life. At the time I was in a church that was very open to the Holy Spirit, and in fact I had been filled with the Spirit the previous year and led others to experience the same. But this church taught that infant baptism and confirmation were the same as the baptism of believers. I can remember explaining to the speaker (probably quite arrogantly) and to one or two of the young people that it was not necessary.

The speaker at the camp did not argue with me. He simply pointed out from Mark 16:15–16 and Acts 18:8 that the Bible seems to indicate we believe first and are then baptised. Then he said something that the Holy Spirit used to challenge and upset my understanding: "You can stay where you are and stay in that mindset, and God will bless you because He is like that. Or you can be like Peter and jump out of the boat to find out what it will be like to follow Jesus. It can be scary, but it is worth it for the adventure of your life."

I knew he was right. God is gracious and will deal with us wherever we are. But if we really want to follow Him closely, to discover what some of the saints have found, if we really want to be "conquerors" (Revelation 2 and 3), then we need to trust Him and follow closely wherever He leads us. For me, the key issue was what other people would think if I were to be baptised.

So, I immediately spoke to those I had told baptism was not necessary and explained I had repented and changed my mind and would be baptised at the first opportunity. It was a little embarrassing but more than worth it. The opportunity came sooner than I expected, because we decided to hold baptisms at the camp itself. On 13th August 1976, under a grey sky and in a strong breeze, I was baptised in the sea in South Devon. I knew it was a significant sign of the fact I had repented and become a Christian. I did not realise at the time quite how significant it was.

Over the following months and years, I started to see that something more happens at baptism than meets the eye. In Romans 6:1–14, Paul explains that baptism is a burial of the old way of life. Just as Jesus rose from the dead, so we can live with a newness of life even now, before our own death and resurrection at the Last Day. In baptism, "we have been united with him in a death like his," Paul says in verse 5. This is a spiritual truth and speaks of a spiritual event, not just a natural event of going into a pool (or the sea in my case) or having water poured or sprinkled over someone who has come to believe and trust in Jesus. Something happens in the spirit realm when we are baptised.

The theological term for this is 'sacrament,' a word based on a Latin word for oath or something pledged by oath; it came to be adopted in the church context to describe the physical acts that have spiritual significance. The Orthodox churches tend to use the word 'mystery' (*mysterion* in Greek) to describe the same sacraments. Both words suggest that there is something tangible that expresses a spiritual reality that is hidden or mysterious to the purely natural mind. Another way of describing a sacrament is as an earthly, human practice that carries special spiritual significance. In other words, it is not just a sign but a spiritual reality in the form of something natural.

Many Evangelicals and Pentecostals regard baptism and the Lord's Supper as the only sacraments and as merely symbols or representations. They perform the actions because they are commanded to do so in scripture, but without much enthusiasm because they see baptism as merely a sign of conversion and the communion as merely a memorial of the Cross.

The essence of a symbol is that one thing represents or implies or suggests another. Sacramental understandings are crucially different. The scholar Hans Boersma sums up the difference: "Unlike mere symbols, sacraments actually participate in the mysterious reality to which they point."[9] This, like the Orthodox emphasis on all of life being open to grace, resonates with Pentecostals and Charismatics (like the All Nations family), who seek to "pray without ceasing" (1 Thessalonians 5:17) and welcome the presence of God by the Spirit in all aspects of life. We do not have to become Catholics or Orthodox in our thinking and practice but are enriched when we appreciate what our Catholic and Orthodox brothers and sisters have embraced from the scriptures: the life-changing potential of the sacraments.

The old way of life is buried in baptism: it is the theological basis (the *legal* basis, if you like) for living free from sinful attitudes. When John says, "I am writing these things to you so that you may not sin" (1 John 2:1), he really means it because he is writing to believers who have been baptised and are filled with the Spirit. The sacrament opens our lives

---

[9] **See Boersma *Heavenly Participation* p. 23**

up to God's Spirit in a new way, so we have the potential to live being filled and led by the Spirit.

Baptism is "into Christ" and is also the basis for freedom from demonic influences (Colossians 2:9–15). I have come across people who were set free from various demonic holds as they were baptised. Of course, as always, the Kingdom is both here among us and is coming: we live in the overlap between this present evil age and the age to come. We have experienced something of the powers of the age to come and we pray for the advance of the Kingdom (Jesus' reign) here on earth as it is in the heavenly places. But the fulness of the Kingdom will come when He returns and at the resurrection on the Last Day. Because in baptism we identify with Jesus in His death and resurrection, baptism in water opens the way for us to experience more of the age to come.

Finally, a very significant aspect of baptism is that if we are baptised into Christ, then we are baptised into His Body, the church. Not just a local church with the disciples who are baptising but into the whole worldwide church made up of all who follow Jesus. Paul refers to the Old Testament people of God as "baptised into Moses" (1 Corinthians 10:2) and uses their experience of passing through the Red Sea as a symbol of baptism that emphasises this fact: it is to do with becoming part of the whole people of God. In the

Old Testament, circumcision was the sign of becoming a part of the People, but this was by definition only for males. Now, baptism is the sign of the new covenant and is open to male and female alike.

In Galatians 3:27–29, Paul makes clear that if we are baptised into Christ, we are clothed with Him and therefore are no longer defined by the human distinctions between people. Baptism gives us a new heredity. We are included among Abraham's offspring and therefore in the covenant promises to Abraham. Belonging to Christ is what defines us and is a higher loyalty than any other earthly characteristic.

11. God's gifts: Forgiveness

Amidst all the noise and confusion on the day of Pentecost as described in Acts 2, Peter stood up and explained. He preached the first ever evangelistic sermon, which can be summarised as, "Jesus is Lord. What are you going to do about it?" As we have seen, there are two parts to the response: repent, and be baptised. Repentance is mainly an internal response of heart and mind but has very practical consequences that can be seen by others. Baptism is mainly an external act that can be seen by others but has a very significant effect spiritually and therefore affects every aspect of who we are as people.

Now we come to the second part of Acts 2:38. There are two things that God does in response to the two things that we have to do: "Repent, and be baptized every one of you in the name of Jesus Christ," Peter says, "so that your sins may be forgiven; and you will receive the gift of the Holy Spirit."

God forgives us. The gospel message includes forgiveness. There is more in the gospel, but this is a vital start.

Our sin, or independence, has made a separation between us and God, between us and other people, between us and the creation and therefore within ourselves; we are suffering alienation in all these ways. The Bible presents different ways of understanding what theologians call atonement or reconciliation between us and God. Whichever is our preferred understanding, the atonement has a dramatic effect in reversing all the aspects of alienation. We can be at home with God, ourselves, others and (ultimately, when the new creation is completed) with the creation. As a result, we can even be reconciled with ourselves and experience a peace that only God can give.

The New Testament uses some different metaphors or symbols to explain the atonement, listed below.

- A ransom or redemption ("buy back") (Mark 10:45; Acts 20:28; Titus 2:14)

- New covenant (Luke 22:20)

- Healing (John 3:14–15; 1 Peter 2:24)

- Self-sacrifice (John 12:23–26)

- Victory (John 12:31–33; Colossians 2:13–15)

- Revelation or unveiling of God's love (John 3:16 and 12:45)

- Substitution or exchange (Galatians 3:13; 2 Corinthians 5:21)

- New creation (2 Corinthians 5:17)

Each of these is found clearly in scripture, but each can lead to problems if the metaphor is pushed too far. For example, if the Cross was paying a ransom, who needs to receive the payment? Or if it is a sacrifice, how exactly did it work and does that make too much separation between Father and Son, when we know that all three Persons are the one God and were present at the Cross? Or if it is an unveiling of God's love, does salvation happen automatically?

As I said in Chapter 2, these metaphors all express an element of the truth, but some are more significant than others. We must view atonement not in a dispassionate, academic way but in relationship with Jesus. I believe we experience atonement primarily as God's victory through His own unique self-sacrifice (rather than because of His infinite power). This avoids too much emphasis on who pays what price or ransom to whom and keeps the attention on giving glory to God. I believe this gives proper weight to the various metaphors, including what has been called 'penal substitution,' the concept that Jesus' self-sacrifice was a penalty necessary to achieve redemption.

Whatever our understanding, the important question is: "How can we receive this salvation?" By 'redemptive participation.' In other words, we are redeemed as we participate in Christ. This is initially through baptism in water and the Spirit, both energised by repentance and faith.

But then we continue to abide in Him. So, we are made righteous when we respond to Him but continue to be made righteous as we continue to live in Him. Righteousness is at the same time a past, present and future experience of being in right relationship with God.

The Hebrew understanding of atonement was to do with those who were excluded from the people of God being re-included with the people. The emphasis is on relationship rather than legal language. I recognise that different conclusions are drawn by many sincere, Spirit-filled believers who read scripture as their inspiration. There is value in thinking through the issues raised by the different metaphors and concepts listed in the Appendix, and we need to be self-aware enough to understand how we are biased and why we come to particular conclusions. But at the end of the day, what matters is to encounter Jesus, acknowledge Him as Lord and receive the gift of forgiveness made possible because of the Cross.

12. God's gifts: The Spirit brings us into the family

The second promise Peter made to those who would respond on the day of Pentecost was "you shall receive the gift of the Holy Spirit" (Acts 2:38). In other words, you will receive what we have just received.

To many people, the word 'spirit' produces an image of something wispy and insubstantial, like smoke or mist. It can be seen and felt but not identified or grasped. The cartoon image of a spirit is more like a white blob, and countless children have used a sheet to dress up as a ghost. In most parts of the world other than the West, most people have a very real appreciation of the spiritual forces at work in the world, often with deep-rooted fear of evil spirits that need to be placated.

To the Jews who were in Jerusalem for the feast of Pentecost, Peter's words would have reminded them of the Spirit of God promised in the Old Testament. Not only promised but also experienced by those Old Testament forebears like David or the many prophets speaking under the inspiration of the Spirit. They would have recalled the oil poured over the priests as a sign of the Spirit or an invitation to God to consecrate them.

Wind, fire, water and oil are all images used in scripture to describe the Holy Spirit. But there is one image that is perhaps more fundamental: the root meaning of both the Hebrew *ruach* and Greek *pneuma* is 'wind' or 'breath.'

The primary way to describe the Son is 'Word' — God is communicating Himself through the Son. The primary way to describe the Spirit is 'breath,' all the more mysterious because it is less obvious to human sight. God is acting through the Spirit but we see only the effects, not the Person or nature of the Spirit.

On that day, Peter could refer his listeners to what they had seen and heard. This was a dramatic experience as the breath of God blew on the disciples. There was a sound like a mighty wind and the fire of God was visible to the eye (Acts 2:2–3): there was no doubt that power was present. Nor was there any doubt that God was at work. They might not have been able to explain it all, but the onlookers had to admit there was something dramatic going on that was spiritual and outside their experience.

Whether we come from a rationalist background, sceptical of any spiritual dimension, or a New Age, pagan or religious background that recognises spirituality in some way, the effect of the Holy Spirit at work has to be reckoned with.

The events of Pentecost 2,000 years ago and similar experiences today cannot just be explained away as make-belief.

There are two aspects that seem to stand out about the experience of the early church in Acts. First, that their initial baptism in the Spirit was a corporate experience, and second that every account of being filled with the Spirit in the New Testament seems to imply an experience that is so tangible, it becomes obvious to those around. I suggest both these are significant and normative for the church in all ages, however different the contexts and cultural assumptions might be.

The Spirit's coming at Pentecost was not just a blessing for the individuals but actually formed the church. Pentecost was the birth of the church, but it was not just a first and unique experience that needed to be so dramatic to "kick-start" the church. It was first in time but not unique.

The Spirit's continued coming in power today is not just a blessing and inspiration or a reason for unbelievers to come to faith as they witness miracles happen. As the Spirit works among us, we continue to be formed into the church. As individuals and as small, related communities, we are transformed into Jesus' likeness by the Spirit who joins our hearts and lives together.

Furthermore, Pentecost is the paradigm or key example of how people can receive the Holy Spirit. Much of our experience in the church has been rather tame: a feeling of peace and release into praying in an unlearned heavenly language. Or it may be a sense of anointing for purpose and supernatural leading in prayer, with occasional miraculous answers. We do not want to minimise or disparage these experiences. They are real and significant for those who begin to know the presence of God through the Spirit in these ways. However, there is more.

The problem is that we rarely look for and long for more, when even the pages of the New Testament give examples of radically life-changing experiences or imply that being filled with the Spirit is so dramatic that it becomes obvious to onlookers. In Acts 8, Philip preached the Good News in Samaria and did miracles; many responded but there was something missing. The apostles in Jerusalem heard about it and sent Peter and John to see what was happening; but they needed to lay hands on the disciples and pray for them to be filled with the Spirit (verses 14–16).

What was missing? Perhaps it was as simple as praying in tongues as many classic Pentecostals might assume, but it is more likely to be the sort of radical changes of lifestyle that had been evident in Jerusalem in Acts 2:42–47 and Acts 4:32–37.

Baptism in the Spirit is transformative and can be so dramatic that it is obvious whether someone has been filled or not. Whether it is the miracle of being motivated by love to give away valuable possessions, or miracles of healing or deliverance, there *have* to be miracles, and not just supernatural experiences but miracles that build community. When the Spirit comes upon people as described in Acts, disciples do not stay isolated individuals but are joined together. If we experience the Holy Spirit in the same sort of way as the New Testament believers, then a church comes into being when the Spirit comes. Community life springs up and communities are formed.

I became a follower of Jesus, of sorts, from the age of about 10 but only discovered fellowship as a teenager. I had attended a Christian youth club faithfully since the age of 10, with some encouragement from my parents who did not belong to a church and were not religious but saw the benefit of me having some involvement with friends outside school. But as a sixteen-year-old, I started to connect with others in prayer and fellowship, particularly two Christian school friends.

The subject of baptism in the Spirit was new, live and being discussed. Some others we knew had experienced something of the Spirit, and when my two friends discovered that I had read a book about it a few months earlier, they wanted me to explain and pray for them to be filled. I sounded characteristically confident in passing on what I had read and learned (I trust I have learned some humility in the decades since then). But what happened surprised me. It was not exactly as described in the book.

My own experience after reading the book had been to ask to be filled, to believe God would answer and to start praying in an unlearned language. I duly did so, and it seemed peaceful but not dramatic. In fact, after a few months I had stopped using the gift of praying in tongues. When I prayed for my friends, there was still peace but also great joy and uncontrollable laughter as we experienced the joy of the Holy Spirit together as we prayed. All three of us prayed in tongues, as I recall, but also a prophetic word was shared. The real surprise, though, was the clear sense we had that this was a corporate baptism in the Spirit. God was joining our hearts and we felt Him speak to us about using us together as a team in helping others become disciples. Over the next few years, we did indeed see that happen. As the Spirit came, we were being formed into a team, not a church as such at that stage, but definitely a team.

Our experience of being filled was not unique. All over the world and in all ages, there have been disciples discovering, as the first Christians did, that the Spirit comes on us as small groups of people to form us into His household.

One individual cannot contain and express the life of God because God Himself is three Persons and it is the love between them that is His nature. Although an individual can worship in Spirit and truth, only a community can be a "temple" to host His presence in a context of worship.

The glorious church life described at the end of Acts 2 was the result. It was a foretaste of the new creation that had begun as the Spirit came to bring the life of Jesus. When forgiven, we are reconciled to God and with ourselves. When filled with the Spirit, we begin a process of being reconciled to one another and the whole creation. The implications of that simple question, "What must we do?" are way beyond our imagination.

13. Hear and obey

The continuing work of the Spirit in our lives has very obvious consequences day to day. From the start, the new Christians of the first church "devoted themselves" to four things that had a background history in their Old Testament Jewish faith but were transformed by the effect of the Spirit in their lives. They are 1) the apostles' teaching, 2) fellowship, 3) breaking bread and 4) prayer (or 'the prayers'). We will look at these four things in this and the next three chapters.

Teaching is one of those words that can bring up all sorts of unhelpful memories or assumptions. Many people sadly have had unfortunate experiences of school and associate teaching with failing to understand or achieve, or perhaps being made to feel small and insignificant. We all think we know what teaching in a church context is, but we usually make assumptions very different from scripture.

What did the first disciples devote themselves to? What was it that was so attractive and compelling in the apostles' teaching? It was not just theory or ideas, but truths lived out in practice and modelled for the hearers.

No doubt the apostles in the early days had first-hand recollections of Jesus' life and ministry. As they repeated what they had heard and seen, some of their hearers who could read and write would take notes. That is how the Gospels came to be written: Matthew, Mark, Luke and John were inspired by the Spirit as they wrote down what the apostles and those close to them were saying (also inspired by the Spirit). Where possible, they recorded the actual words of Jesus (who of course was also inspired by the Spirit as He spoke). Perhaps Peter deliberately asked Mark to make a record, but in any case, that Gospel has always been associated with Peter. It was likely that Luke was part of Paul's team and relied on what had been passed on through many others, but it is clear from the way he wrote (and from Luke 1:1–4) that he was methodical and checked his sources.

What we now know as the four Gospels consist of a core part of what the apostles passed on and taught. And there are certainly many ideas and even philosophical statements in them (particularly in John). Jesus said in Matthew 5 several times "You have heard it said…. But I say to you…." Ideas have to be communicated in words that are said or written. But they are not just ideas. What Jesus said, He expects us to obey. Just as He incarnated the nature of God in human form, so we need to put into practice — to incarnate — what He says to us.

This emphasis on "hear and obey," not just "hear," runs throughout the scriptures. In fact, to Hebrew minds, it was impossible to use the word "hear" without implying the response, usually that it must be obeyed. The concepts of "hear" and "obey" are so closely related in the Hebrew word *shema* that it can be translated into English as either of these words. The Greek culture was different, and the Greek word for "hear" used in the New Testament means simply to hear and usually to process what is heard; there is a separate Greek word for obey, which refers to acting upon what is heard.

Jesus' teaching, and that of the apostles, is about action, putting into practice what is said. In Acts 1:1, Luke begins his account of the early church by referring to what Jesus began "to *do* and to teach." Jesus taught out of His own life and lifestyle: He first demonstrated and then explained. There are many indications that the apostles did exactly the same.

Decades after the first outpouring of the Spirit at Pentecost, Paul explained that he and others with him were experiencing trouble and taking up the cross daily, identifying with the death of Jesus, "so that the life of Jesus may be made visible in our mortal flesh" (2 Corinthians 4:11). They preached and taught in words that were inspired by the Spirit and would therefore produce life in others if received and obeyed; but just as importantly they demonstrated this eternal life in their mortal bodies. On some occasions, it was through miracles. At other times, it was through showing patient endurance and forgiveness under severe persecution. But at all times, the life of Jesus was displayed in their lives and character. This is why Paul encouraged his hearers to imitate him or follow his example. (1 Corinthians 11:1; Philippians 3:17 and 4:9; 2 Thessalonians 3:7)

There are many Old Testament examples of teaching: Ezra the priest, who with helpers explained the Law to the exiles who returned to Jerusalem (Nehemiah 8:1–8), or the prophets, who explained as well as declared or acted out a prophetic message. But the main significance of the Old Testament background to this new development, the formation of the church, is that the apostles only had the Hebrew scriptures to teach from. There are clues throughout the New Testament of how they did so, finding Jesus in the Old Testament scriptures and using them in symbolic ways to express the gospel. They ran the risk of opening up differing interpretations as they did this, but it was a journey of exploration inspired by the Spirit to find Jesus throughout the Hebrew scriptures.

Many Christians throughout the ages have been so anxious to preserve the truth of scripture that they can be very critical of those who think about or express it using different words or concepts. The sad fact is that if we think of truth, or sound doctrine, as only ideas and words, then we will inevitably define it in such a way that we exclude many others. A theoretical approach always leads to division and breaking unity. In contrast, when we hear and obey, we know what really matters: the goal of teaching is love (1 Timothy 1:5). There can be many different ways of expressing the truth that Jesus is both fully God and fully human, for example, and people have argued about whether He had one nature or two and how the divine and human are related. But there is no doubt that the New Commandment He gave is to love one another. It is unequivocal. As Mark Twain confessed, "It ain't those parts of the Bible that I can't understand that bother me, it is the parts that I do understand."[10] Theory leads to division, but abiding in Jesus — making Him central — allows the Spirit to work in us and develop unity.

The parable of the wise and foolish builders (Matthew 7:24–27) is a stern warning to act on what we hear. Jesus also taught," If you continue in my word, you are truly my disciples, and you will know the truth, and the truth will set you free" (John 8:31–32).

---

[10] **Quote is largely attributed to Mark Twain, e.g. John R. W. Stott** *Christ the Liberator* **p. 214**

His invitation to us is to live in His word, to live in conversation with Him, in intimate relationship. The implication is that we obey what He says, and the promise is that if we do so, we will know the truth.

Truths from scripture and prophetic promises or warnings are not just ideas to inform us or dramatic inspiration to entertain us. If they stay merely in our thinking, they are useless. "But be doers of the word, and not hearers only…" (James 1:22), the Bible says, or else we are in deception. It is when we put the truth of scripture into practice and actively respond to the prophetic that we find the Kingdom coming more and more in our lives.

The truth is not ultimately a set of ideas or philosophy. It cannot be defined in words. The ultimate Truth is a Person, Jesus. And when we embrace truth, it takes on flesh — it becomes incarnated in us — as we receive from Jesus by the Spirit. When we are in close fellowship with Jesus, His words become "flesh" in our lives. We are changed by His words so others can see Him in us.

When we hear each other, the same Holy Spirit who inspires the speaker is speaking to us in our hearts. In 1 Corinthians 2:6–13, Paul explains this in almost mystical terms. When we receive what is said, not just as ideas or practical instructions but as inspired by God, there is a spiritual impartation that causes things to change in our lives. That is why it is so important to be discerning and to receive wholeheartedly what is from God and not allow anything to get mixed in with it, such as human ideas or something that comes from a wrong motivation (1 John 4:1–6). So, let's receive these things and put them into practice. Like the first disciples, let's devote ourselves to the apostles' teaching.

14. Together

The first disciples devoted themselves to fellowship. They were like an extended family or a network of many extended families. They spent time together in various ways and we get a glimpse of their lifestyle in Acts 2:42–47. They not only shared time together in the Temple and in homes, they were also grateful and generous people. They shared food, possessions and finances. As we shall see in the next chapter, sharing food was both a way of developing friendship and a sacramental way of celebrating and inviting the presence of God among them in the act of breaking bread. But fellowship is seen in many other contexts.

We use the word a lot in Christian circles, but what is 'fellowship?' At its simplest, the word speaks of being together or companionship and sharing in something together. It overlaps with 'friendship' but is broader because we can be joined together in fellowship with people we do not naturally like or would not naturally link with. In fact, God delights in joining former enemies together. When people from hostile backgrounds are united in love, they proclaim by their actions the reconciliation that is at the heart of the gospel. God's cosmic purpose is for all people and all things (the whole creation) to be reconciled to Him.

Every time enemies are reconciled in Jesus, He is glorified and the world has a prophetic sign of this complete reconciliation to come.

The word fellowship used in the Old Testament has a particular significance in the 'fellowship offering' or 'peace offering', which is introduced in Leviticus 3 and explained in more detail in Leviticus 7. A worshipper would make this offering as a spontaneous or freewill offering to express particular thanks to God. For example, Hannah did so as part of fulfilling her vow to bring Samuel to the Temple. It was a way of saying she was at peace with God and herself and was holding nothing back in fulfilling her vow. Other types of sacrifices were to cover sin. In fact, the sin offering would be the first of the day and the fellowship offerings would be laid on top of the altar while the fire was still burning, as a sign that we have peace and fellowship on the basis of our sin being forgiven so that our relationship with God is restored. The fat and kidneys were the parts of the animal laid on the fire, symbolising that part of the sacrifice was somehow consumed by the Lord. Then certain parts of the animal were given to the priest for him and his family to eat, while the rest was for the worshipper's family and friends to eat. It is a picture of sharing and enjoying food together.

Perhaps the earliest Christians in Jerusalem were often in the Temple for two different reasons. It was certainly a convenient place for a larger number to gather. But the daily worship and sacrifices also provided continual reminders of the way Jesus had offered Himself as the Lamb of God. He was both the High Priest and the sacrifice. He was the sacrifice for sin and also the sacrifice for fellowship or thanksgiving offerings because it is Jesus' resurrection life that we share.

The New Testament word for fellowship has a root meaning of sharing together in something bigger. Two or more people share in something that is outside their lives and more significant than them. As Christians, we share first and foremost in Jesus. This sharing has radical consequences.

The early Christians were often persecuted. Among the many inspiring examples of faith and perseverance is the story of the martyrdom of Perpetua and Felicitas, who were killed by wild beasts in the amphitheatre in Carthage in 203 AD along with four men. They were young in years and young in the faith as they were all preparing for baptism. They were actually baptised in prison, where their teacher voluntarily joined them and died with them — that gives those of us who teach something to think about.

Perpetua was well born and literate. She wrote an account of their time in prison. The others were either slaves or low born. This in itself was a tremendous witness as they stood in front of the crowd and shared the kiss of peace with one another: it rocked the worldview of the status-conscious Romans, who lived in a stratified society. Perpetua and her fellow disciples knew they were family together, and their family bond, formed by the Holy Spirit, was more important than anything inherited from their Roman worldview.

If we all seek to put Jesus first in our lives, we will find ourselves sharing together in Him, and the Spirit of Jesus will join us together spiritually. We also share in some very practical, down-to-earth things, like eating together or being in the same place together or doing something together. The spiritual reality needs to be expressed in very ordinary ways.

Even for those who are not disciples, friendship and fellowship grow when the emphasis is on being together. It might be taking part in a hobby or just helping an acquaintance do some decorating, but doing things together is the best way of growing any friendship.

Some of my closest friends are people we walk with. When Catherine and I were leading a church-planting team in Kirkby-in-Ashfield, in the East Midlands, we would often take tents and caravans and travel into Derbyshire for a weekend, just an hour's drive away. By "we," I mean most of the team and others who were connected with us, some of whom were Christians and some not. Friendships grew as we enjoyed cups of tea in the camping field (or each other's caravans or tents in the pouring rain, as frequently happened). Friendships grew as we walked in the Peak District hills and dales and shared picnics, or donned wellies and waterproofs and braved the weather. It is easier to talk about things that matter in life when you are sharing experiences and relaxing out of doors.

We moved away from that area in 1996, but since that time we and two other families in particular have stayed in touch to meet, to walk and talk together in the hills and to share our lives. Our friendship has deepened because we have made time to walk and talk over the years. Likewise, fellowship develops when we share in Him spiritually and also take time to listen and talk with each other, and simply to be together. For much of our lives, Catherine and I have tried to live within walking distance of many of our key Christian friends. But it is not always possible to live so close geographically, and that means we need to be intentional and make more effort to stay in close and meaningful contact.

15. Around the table

The first Christians devoted themselves to breaking bread, Acts 2:42 tells us. Bread was the basis of every meal and 'breaking bread' is a way of saying 'sharing a meal.' Eating together has very high importance in the Middle East and also in many Asian and African cultures. It is not just about fuelling the body while in the same space as other individuals. It is a sharing of the whole person in intimacy with those who share the meal. An invitation to eat together honours the guest and speaks of acceptance, alliance and close friendship. People who eat together belong together. We see a picture in Acts 2:42 of the first Christians breaking bread together, which would have involved doing just this — sharing a meal in a relaxed and intimate way.

Jesus Himself hosted dinner parties during His earthly ministry (in Mark 2:15, there is a suggestion from the conversation that Jesus was the host even though they were in Levi's house). And of course, there are other occasions mentioned where He was invited by someone specifically named. The Middle Eastern worldview dictated that you only invite family and close friends to eat with you, but Jesus invited people who were enemies and socially unacceptable. To make matters more difficult, the Pharisees tried to live with great purity at the meal table, as if they were priests.

The preparation of the food and the "holiness" of all at the meal were therefore very important. By inviting outcasts of various kinds to share dinner with Him, Jesus was not only breaking the norm of just inviting family and close friends, He was also bringing in "pollution" by having people who were not ritually clean according to the Law.

The apostles remembered this — how could they forget? — and taught the early church to welcome *all people* who want to gather around Jesus. In Acts 2:46, we find they broke bread at home, literally "from home to home." The word order emphasises this because it was radical: it implies that everyone who was a disciple of Jesus could be both an honoured guest and a generous host. We are family, not guests. In church, we all belong, and this is beautifully expressed around the table, in intimate fellowship with a few. Typically, homes were very small, and it could be crowded even with four or five guests, but numbers are not the issue here. Everyone belongs somewhere, and if all disciples are gathering in small groups, there are many who are connected by the Spirit. Everyone can host and be hosted because this is not just hospitality, it is sharing the life of the Holy Spirit.

Set against this rich background, our celebration of Holy Communion or the Lord's Supper today can seem rather sombre and religious. Why? I suggest it is because we focus on how we do it, what we say and trying to get it "right." Instead, let's focus on the Person of Jesus and remember Him, as He commanded in Luke 22:19. Worship and prayer spring up naturally in the context of a shared meal, and we echo the early church who "ate their food with glad and generous hearts" (Acts 2:46). Even in larger gatherings, when the Person of Jesus is the focus, sharing communion together can become a dynamic context for the Holy Spirit to move among us.

Breaking bread is one of the main ways that God has provided for us to meet with Him. It reinforces the whole gospel story and reminds us of our dependence on Him at all times. It is, Paul teaches in 1 Corinthians 10:16–17, a celebration of what Jesus has done and a sign of our unity and fellowship. Jesus reveals Himself by the Holy Spirit as we share and break the bread, if we "discern the body" (1 Corinthians 11:29), which means both welcoming Jesus to be present by His Spirit and recognising we are part of His Body the church.

Over the years, from when our children were still very young, we have prayed and remembered Jesus at the meal table with the family and with whoever is with us for a meal. Catherine and I usually break bread every day at the main meal. We have experimented with various ways of praying and worshipping. Sometimes it is very short —

as short as a simple thanksgiving for the meal but specifically welcoming Jesus to the table and remembering the Cross and resurrection. Sometimes we have carried on praying and giving thanks and praise at length during the meal, letting the conversation flow from one topic to another, sometimes as ordinary conversation, sometimes turning naturally into prayer and involving God very directly.

We have used bread or biscuits or any simple food that can be shared. Scholars have found that bread and wine were the basic nutrition for meals all around the Mediterranean, and on many days some poor people might have nothing else, other than a few herbs to flavour the bread.[11] Wealthier people would add all kinds of foods, but these were still based on bread and wine. In the UK, wine might be replaced by tea as the almost-universal drink. It really does not matter what we use provided our hearts are clean and worshipful. My preference is to break the bread or whatever we are using while together rather than share anything already broken, because it is such a powerful sign of being one body in the Spirit as we share the same item of food.

---

[11] See McGowan *Ancient Christian Worship* pp. 22-23

In our everyday life, the natural place to break bread in a special way to remember Jesus is in the home. We find in Matthew 26:26–29, Luke 22:19 and 1 Corinthians 11:23–26 that the command was first given to His friends at the Last Supper, which was a Passover meal. This was a feast to celebrate and remember the deliverance from Egypt by the blood of the sacrificial lambs. Breaking bread together is a way of remembering, but with the expectation that Jesus would be present ("This is my…" He said, not "This is like my…"). It is also an anticipation of the heavenly banquet, the wedding feast of the Lamb (Revelation 21:1–8).

John Wesley taught that communion was "a saving ordinance" through which people could encounter God, although many other teachers in church history have regarded it as for Christians only. In almost any expression of church as people gather, it is hard to say whether a person is currently living in faith or responding to Jesus. Even if they have been doing so in the past, they may now be in rebellion or living with unconfessed sin or simply not trusting actively in Jesus and following the Spirit. In the Gospels, every person who encountered Jesus was either moving towards Him or away from Him: there is no static position in relation to God. However, if the prayers and declarations include a simple re-telling of the whole story or of the gospel message, then opportunity is given for anyone to respond to Jesus in their heart in the moment.

In our own experience of breaking bread with a small group, I recall a time when someone who was close to deciding to follow Jesus was with us for the meal. He was very glad to be included and keen to hear about the significance of praying and sharing a piece of bread. This led to a great opportunity to explain the gospel in 60 seconds and to invite him to take part if he would like to — he actually chose not to (possibly showing he had sensed something of the presence of God) but a few weeks later decided to follow Jesus.

Even though it is so significant, it is good to keep Holy Communion simple, natural and non-religious. All that is needed is to pray, giving thanks and inviting the presence of Jesus, preferably after reading or reminding ourselves of a passage of scripture. Of course, there may be other things the Spirit inspires you to pray, but there is a warning in 1 Corinthians 11:17–34. If we have anything against a brother or sister, then we must sort it out first because breaking bread is a declaration of unity and an invitation to the Risen Lord to be present by His Spirit. He is holy and is particularly firm in His instruction about forgiving (the only part of the model outline prayer He gave, the Lord's Prayer, which He emphasised and explained:

Matthew 6:14–15). Even around a lively meal table where young children help keep things down to earth, do not take the Lord's presence lightly.

16. Around the throne

The first disciples devoted themselves to prayer. They were passionate about praying together as well as on their own.

Many of us have an image of prayer as difficult or forced, maybe because of difficult experiences of prayer meetings or just because we do not think we are praying enough or as we should. There is a lot that can be said about prayer and many books have been written — some are really outstanding, many good and some not so helpful. But we often read the books or the examples of praying saints not as encouragement but as a standard to achieve. If so, we fear we are not doing enough.

It is good to encourage and challenge one another to pray more, but not in a way that makes us feel we are failing. So let us start with the basis of all praying: God loves us and takes the initiative in offering us His friendship. Friendship, as we have seen already, is at the heart of the gospel. God's intention was, from the very beginning of time, for finite human beings, stuck in time, to have friendship with the infinite God who is outside time.

Prayer is not complex but is simply talking with God, and that includes listening to Him. Prayer is having a conversation. What can make it seem complicated or difficult is that God is infinite and outside time. He is spirit, so we connect with Him in spirit, not just in ordinary human ways. But He has taken the initiative and enables us to connect with Him. As we use ordinary human words, thoughts, actions, pictures or just stay quiet, the God who is spirit comes and gives them spiritual effect. He responds to our feeble attempts and uses the same sort of human means to communicate with us. He speaks by His Spirit into that part of us which is spiritual and our powerful but finite minds then find ways of interpreting it in ideas, thoughts, pictures and impressions. All this is possible because Jesus opened the way for us to know God and to become righteous and holy, like He is. The Cross and resurrection open up the possibility of intimate communication.

So, the basis of prayer is not that we try to get into God's presence or try to become something we are not. That is religion — self-help and trying to reach the sky. Not only does it not work but it actually angers God because religion seeks to replace His grace with our effort. In Jesus, God took the initiative to come close to us. He opened the way for us to become friends of God. So, if we try to get to God by our own effort, we are being religious. And religion is based on independence, and independence is the essence of sin.

Instead, our praying is based on the fact that we can be in God's presence, sensing His holiness without being burned to a cinder, because Jesus makes us holy and righteous. It is based on God's initiative and His desire to develop friendship with us.

Prayer is not based on our understanding. How can we even imagine that God can have an intimate friendship with billions of people at the same time? Yet prayer is not completely illogical or beyond us. It is simply having a conversation.

There are some practical things we can do to facilitate conversation. It is usually helpful to talk out loud to God. And it helps to give plenty of time to Bible reading, silence and worship so we can hear Him speak in our spirit, mediated through the mind but often without conscious thought. I find it much easier to listen to God and to talk with Him while walking. Maybe it is because the fresh air and exercise are enjoyable. Maybe it is because my mind is not directly focused on a time frame, so there is a more relaxed atmosphere. Or perhaps it is just the way I am.

One thing is clear from many of the books about praying and the example of many saints renowned for their praying: when we grow in our knowledge and understanding of God, we experience His friendship more and more. We have more to talk about together. And we can enjoy each other's company in silence more as well. As we develop our friendship with God, we also become devoted to prayer.

The first disciples prayed as they shared meals together from house to house. I have the impression it was informal, and people prayed whatever they felt able to pray or wanted to pray. Yet there is more in the simple words of Acts 2:42: literally, it says they devoted themselves "to prayer" or "to the prayers."

Like most religions, the Jewish faith that developed from the Old Testament people of God used some set prayers. They were based on the scriptures, but by the time of Jesus, the scholars ("scribes") and other rabbis had developed some set prayers or liturgies. Why? If we are religious (in the bad sense of being independent of God), it is because we think it will help us get to God or make our praying effective. But if we use set prayers in faith because we are responding to God's unconditional love for us and want to deepen our friendship with Him, then they can be very helpful. They can help us express our adoration, our hopes and longings for others and ourselves.

These words have been carefully and prayerfully prepared. Sometimes I use prayers that are in the Church of England liturgy because I am familiar with them, or from other sources. There is a wealth of material available to us. I also use some prayers I have written, often as a result of being challenged by God and wanting to pray something regularly to invite Him to change me.

So, set prayers can be helpful in developing friendship, or harmful if we are just being religious. It all depends on our heart attitude. The first Christians were accustomed to reciting certain scriptures and praying certain words based on scripture at fixed times of the day. It is a rhythm or routine that Christians, and later Muslims, adopted. Whatever informal prayers we pray throughout the day, there are certain times during the day when we stop to refocus, worship and ask for help. It can be a helpful thing to do. I have a list of scriptures and some set prayers I have collected for certain different times in the day and use them as a prompt — not every day and not at all the times I have in mind, but sometimes they prompt some refocusing and prayer.

The first Christians would probably have been in this sort of habit, and we also read that they met in the Temple, where there were set prayers twice a day around certain sacrifices, morning and afternoon. One of the intriguing problems we Christians all face is how much of our cultural background we change when we become disciples and how much we continue, though now led and energised by the Spirit.

When we become disciples, we leave the kingdom of darkness and enter the Kingdom of God. It is a complete transformation. But we find ourselves pilgrims in a world hostile to God. And yet God also loves the diverse cultures and the variations of style between different people groups and individuals. He loves our cultural identity. So, we are not only pilgrims, part of a spiritual family in Christ, but we are also placed in the culture and the natural family we grew up in. Those first disciples had to ask God whether they should continue using set prayers or just let words and emotions flow in response to the Spirit's moving among them. Maybe different ones came to different conclusions. I expect so because there was a lot of variety in the next generation.

Whatever other words we use, it is always important to pray using scripture. We can pray God's own words because ours are inadequate. We can pray with the psalmists, using their words but reading them in the light of Jesus, and maybe when we would not otherwise dare to say some of those things to God. When we pray along with Jesus, Paul or one of the other letter writers in the New Testament, we know we are praying what is on God's heart.

So, let's experiment with praying in all contexts and in all ways. But most importantly, let's pray, both on our own and in community with our church family.

17. Around the community

Much of Jesus' teaching is not difficult to understand, just hard to obey. In fact, it is impossible to obey without the help of the Holy Spirit.

Jesus taught that the Law given in the Old Testament was fulfilled in Him because it pointed prophetically towards the expected Messiah and because He demonstrated what it is to live a perfect life. Yet He also taught and demonstrated that He had authority to go beyond the Law. For example, He deliberately broke some of the ritual laws that were supposed to achieve holiness (being like God) because they can never really achieve it. Besides, He was already holy because the Holy Spirit filled and lived in Him.

In the same way, we can be filled with the Holy Spirit who leads us into what is right and gives us the power to do what is right. So, when Jesus summed up the most important element of His teaching, He knew the Spirit would enable us to become more and more able to fulfil it. "Love one another," He said, "as I have loved you." This is the New Commandment given in John 13:34 and repeated in John 15:12–13. It goes beyond the summary of the Law, which is to love God with everything we have and to love our neighbour as we love ourselves (Matthew 22:37–40).

It is an extraordinary statement. We might think that our response to God loving us would be for us to love Him in return. God, however, is infinitely loving and does not just want a response back to Himself but to share love with all His children. The response He requires, above all, is simply that we love one another. It is not hard to understand but it is impossible to do, except as a response to God's love. When we receive His love, communicated to us by the Spirit, we find we are able to love and forgive others. We start to take on the family likeness, becoming more like God Himself.

What does this love look like? As John taught, "...let us love, not in word or speech, but in truth and action" (1 John 3:18). The well-known passage in 1 Corinthians 13 about love sounds very attractive when read at a wedding, but it is full of down-to-earth realities as we seek to put it into practice day by day. "Love is patient," for example, means not being irritated if the other person keeps making the same mistake. I can only be patient if I am living in God's love by the power of the Spirit. Love needs to be real and to be shown in what we do. Love takes action, even if the action is to listen quietly to a grieving or angry person.

One key demonstration of love is generosity. I recall many years ago talking with our small fellowship group about sharing garden tools and helping each other in tasks around the house and garden as part of our exploration of what it means to be a church of the kind seen in the New Testament. We did not get very far, perhaps, but we tried. Catherine and I were blessed by the number of friends from the church who helped us move house or clear an overgrown garden when we moved in. Later, we were blessed when friends from church realised our house had been broken into while we were away on holiday. They cleared up the mess, leaving only flowers as a sign they had been there. In fact, some of the young men in the church stayed overnight while we were away in case the burglars came back. Neighbours notice this kind of caring and sharing. When we came home after that burglary, one neighbour became a follower of Jesus, saying, "No one loves me like this except my Mum!"

Generosity is so much more than contributing money to a good cause. It includes spending time, often our most valuable resource, just to help and support someone else. Love is listening patiently to an older person's stories because they are lonely. Love is sitting up all night with an anxious parent awaiting news of a child involved in an accident. Love is helping someone build a flat-pack wardrobe (why do the adverts always say "Easy" self-assembly?). Love is not fighting back when someone is unkind but demonstrating kindness in return.

Love is taking a present of groceries to a family struggling to buy food.

If we are to love one another, we need to notice one another's needs. I recall one friend, a leader in the church who was often welcoming groups into her home for meetings or for fun gatherings. She only needed to ask once how different individuals liked their tea or coffee. Love is noticing and remembering what pleases other people. Another might be noticing when a person is lonely but putting on a brave face.

We have a long way to go in our practice of love, particularly generosity, if we are to become more like the early church in Acts. They did not cling on to what they had but shared it, even to the extent of selling possessions to share the money (Acts 2:44–45 and 4:32). The result of that lifestyle of loving one another was that great grace was on the whole community, and key leaders like Barnabas were recognised and raised up by God as a response to their generosity. The apostles were able to testify to the resurrection powerfully because their lifestyles demonstrated God's Kingdom.

I am very grateful for the steps we have taken in the church where I belong, and for the generosity shown by so many in reaching out to neighbours and others in the community. But I long for more and am challenged to take a lead in this, because I want to be part of a community that puts into practice what Jesus commanded.

18. God with us

There is one thing that all churches have to have if they are to be regarded as churches: the presence of God.

So far, we have thought about God's love and initiative and our response as individuals. We have considered how our response to the gospel in repenting, believing and being baptised means we are part of the family. And we have looked at the marks of church, what the family looks like. But we now need to dig a bit deeper into what a church actually is and, therefore, what a church is not.

We can quickly dismiss the idea that a church is defined by the building it meets in. Many churches meet in homes or hired halls anyway. It might be harder to dispel the idea that a church is an organisation, and people often think first of a national or international organisation or denomination. It is easy to see the human exterior of church and find similarities with a sports club or company or trade association. But the fact that there are so many denominations and families of churches, like the All Nations Movement, is itself a clue that the church is bigger than and different from any one denomination or network.

So, what is the church in New Testament terms? First, we need to recognise two uses of the word: the universal church made up of all God's people and the small local unit. Paul often wrote about the universal church when addressing small groups of disciples meeting in homes. For example, in Ephesians 3:14–21 he prays for the local churches in Ephesus and its region but also that "together with all the saints" (Ephesians 3:18), they/we would know the love of Christ that is beyond knowledge. It takes the whole church to know God's love.

The whole church inherits and continues in the good of God's promises to the Old Testament patriarchs. In Acts 7:38, Stephen referred to the church or congregation in the wilderness, using the New Testament word for church to describe the whole people of God leaving Egypt to go into the Promised Land. There is not space here to explore the theme properly, but it is important to note there is both continuity and discontinuity (a dramatic new start) between the historical Israelites, the Old Testament people of God, and the church, the New Testament people of God. The promises made to Abraham still stand, but the interpretation is far greater than he or any Old Testament saint could have imagined. The people of God are no longer a particular ethnic group in a particular geography but a worldwide people from every ethnic and cultural group. As Paul said in 1 Corinthians 15:46, it is a case of first the natural, then the spiritual. The church neither replaces the Jewish people nor is it separate from them. The people of God, the true Israel (Romans 2:9), is now made up of Jews and Gentiles.

Another important thing to have in mind is that scripture does not give us clear instructions on how churches should be structured. It teaches some fundamental principles, such as the New Commandment and the importance of leaders embodying godly character. The New Testament also provides some glimpses of how these principles might have been applied in practice in those contexts. But there is no one pattern or model that is appropriate for all circumstances. Rather, God wants to partner with us in exploring creatively what it means to have our citizenship in heaven while connected with people on earth.

When we think of the universal church, it is huge in scope, but when we focus on local churches, we might think of relatively small gatherings. The implication of the New Testament is that some churches might be very small groups of disciples, even just a handful. Paul refers to several people in his letters who host a church in their house (for example, Philemon 1:2), and scholars have suggested a variety of sizes of home and church, including meeting in very small, shared apartments or shared rooms in tenement blocks.

Jesus is recorded as using the word translated 'church' (εκκλησια *ekklesia*) on two occasions. He would probably have spoken Aramaic, the local language, though He may have also spoken Greek, the language of commerce. The Gospel writers used Greek because that was the usual language for most communication across different groups at the time, very much like English is today. In Matthew 16:13–21, Jesus emphasises the authority of the church He will build: the gates of hell shall not stand up against it. He renames Simon as Peter (Πετρος *Petros*, which means rocky, or stone) and states He will build the church on "this rock" (πετρα *petra*). The church is built from living stones, or people who have seen Jesus by revelation, as Peter had just seen and as he later wrote in 1 Peter 2:5. But it is not simply built on Peter and other disciples as individuals: Jesus would have used the Greek word *Petros* instead of *petra* if that was what He meant. Yet it is not some vague, generalised revelation, otherwise He would not have made a point of changing Simon's name to something so closely related. The people who are brought together to form church are those who have been changed into disciples through a revelation of Jesus.

This is confirmed by the usual meaning of the Greek word *ekklesia* as an assembly for a purpose. In Greek culture, it was an assembly of all the free citizens in a city and also the place in the city centre where they would meet. When the Romans occupied the Greek-speaking Mediterranean regions, they extended the meaning. After conquest, the Roman army would rebuild a city or plant a new colonial city in order to "civilise" the native population and make them Roman. The *ekklesia* was the central part of the town or city and also the gathering of the Roman citizens (who might be locals who had become Roman in outlook and legal status).

The second time Jesus used the word is the nearest we have to a definition of church: Matthew 18:20. It is not good English, but the text can be translated literally as "Where there are two or three who have been gathered [or are being gathered] into My Name, there I am…" The words used to describe the gathering suggest movement, and it is movement "into" Jesus' name. In scripture, a person's name usually describes the essence of their character. So, we are gathered together not just geographically into the same space but spiritually and in sanctification (the lifelong process of our character being transformed), to become more like Jesus.

We are built into church when we share together in the life of God. One pastor/theologian put it this way:

> The Christian Church is, in the purpose and intention of God, that community of people who, as a result of their hearing and believing of the gospel, have been enabled to share through Christ in God's own life, and who, as a result, have begun

to share their lives with one another on every level. It is a norm that very few congregations live up to; yet the more they are in Christ and the more the Spirit sets them free, the nearer they come to it.[12]

The essence of church is the presence of God. It does not have to look like a traditional congregation and it might only be two or three people, but they are sharing lives because they have shared together in receiving God's life.

So, church can be defined as the presence of Jesus among His people, who are connected with Him spiritually and called out as a spiritual family to pursue His mission on the earth. We might be a handful around a meal table, but if we are connected to the Head of the Body and open to fellowship with all other members, then we are part of the Army that is partnering with Him to bring the Kingdom down from heaven to earth.

---

[12] See Smail *The Giving Gift: Holy Spirit in Person* p. 183

19. When things go wrong

When we are in close proximity with others, we have more opportunities to build friendship but also to annoy or irritate each other. It does not take long in any family, workplace or church, or indeed any other context for community, for things to cause us irritation or even anger. It is a feature of life as human beings.

We are all on a journey. We are not yet perfect and make mistakes in what we say and how we say it. Sometimes we or others are deliberately manipulative, trying to get people to do or say what we would like them to. Whether it is to get our own way or even for what seems like a good reason, manipulation is always harmful. Sometimes we or others around us are greedy and selfish. Even if we manage to control ourselves, we are faced with choices about how we will react to others when they lose control. It is challenging to live in community.

It is worth the effort, though, of seeking to build community because we are made for friendships and connection. How can we do this? Paul urges us to make "every effort to maintain the unity of the Spirit in the bond of peace" (Ephesians 4:3), and unity is maintained when we both share in Jesus and make sure we spend time together.

To develop fellowship and maintain unity, we need to give attention to both the spiritual and the human aspects.

The spiritual aspects start with the reality that if we are in Christ, then we are joined with brothers and sisters who are also in Christ. We are to *preserve* the unity, not create it. The Holy Spirit, the wind of God, brought creation into existence and breathed life into humankind (Genesis 1:2 and 2:7). The Spirit also breathes the new creation into existence. When we are born again into this new creation, we are joined with others in the Body of Christ.[13] So the Spirit creates the unity and we are to preserve or keep it by cultivating good habits and making wise choices, in partnership or co-operation with the Spirit. It is not a case of the Spirit joining us and then leaving us to continue holding on to unity by our own efforts. Instead, we continue in the same way we began — by faith or trusting in Him. "As you therefore have received Christ Jesus the Lord," Paul writes, "continue to live your lives in him, rooted and built up in him and established in the faith, just as you were taught, abounding in thanksgiving" (Colossians 2:6–7).

The spiritual reality of our oneness in Christ needs to be expressed in practical, visible ways, and we preserve it as we love one another. Love is shown in the choices we make to

---

[13] See John 1:12–13; John 3:5–7; 2 Corinthians 5:17; 1 Corinthians 12:12–13

speak or hold our tongues, to act kindly and show mercy. It might mean overlooking little offences and peacefully challenging more serious ones, so that we "live in the light" (1 John 1:7) with one another and help fellowship to grow. Or it might be making sure we are thoughtful and kind. Or maybe making more time to do some things together.

Time is a key factor. Time in prayer and hearing from God through scripture enables us to love one another, which is impossible without supernatural help. Time with one another enables friendship to grow. Time to listen and share, time to unravel any misunderstanding or to do something together. Time is our most valuable possession and we can show love by giving it away.

There are other spiritual aspects to relationships. Because we live in a fallen world, until we are rescued and born again into a new creation, we are subject to the influence of demonic powers, which continue to affect most of those around us (Ephesians 2:1–3). Even after we are born again, we can be subject to demonic influences through curses, sometimes brought on ourselves by repeated wrong choices. The good news is we can be freed from these through prayer, preferably with a mature Christian believer. But we need to ask the Holy Spirit for discernment and wisdom about the spiritual dimension to relationships.

I remember working some years ago with several non-Christians who were clearly very influenced by demonic forces. The atmosphere seemed to change when they were around. I felt quite intimidated and unable to be myself with one or two of them, including a person who worked for me but always seemed to be trying to manipulate me to do or think various things, often things that contradicted what they had said before. After a period of weeks of struggling to think straight and to talk my way through the difficulties, I had a revelation when Catherine challenged me very simply: "What have you been praying about this?" How could I be so stupid as to try to battle through, just because it was a workplace not the church, when it is so obvious that praying without ceasing (1 Thessalonians 5:17) includes bringing every difficulty into the Lord's presence?

So, I would pray daily before entering the office, asking for God's protection and leading. I declared that in Jesus, I can take authority over demonic influences and forbid them to hinder me. We cannot cast out a spirit from another person or pray for deliverance for them if they are not willing to be set free, but we can take authority in Christ and so remain free ourselves. And the atmosphere changed every time I did this. I would sometimes pray around the office when it was empty after the others had left, asking God to clear the atmosphere and to make it possible for people to receive revelation from Him. When I forgot, I would often have a bad day, but I continued in prayer. He answered, of course.

We ourselves can nurture our relationships through practical kindness and courtesy, love and generosity. One of the most important dynamics that brings together the spiritual and practical is to forgive straight away when we are hurt or wronged. Jesus actually warned us that if we do not forgive others, then we cut ourselves off from God's forgiveness, in the same way that if we judge others, we open ourselves to being judged (Matthew 6:14–15 and 7:1–2).

Forgiving is not a feeling, nor is it forgetting; it is a choice. Any time we are conscious of being hurt or wronged by someone, we need to choose to release and forgive them. And the best way to choose to forgive is to pray for help and then tell God you choose to forgive and ask Him to bless them. No hesitation. No question. No excuses. No debate about "Am I ready to forgive?" Because we will never be ready if we wait until we feel like it. This may seem harsh, but it is quite clear in Jesus' teaching: God cannot forgive us if we withhold forgiveness from a brother or sister.

"How many times do I have to forgive?" asked Peter in Matthew 18:21. The Law said three times. He went further and suggested seven, no doubt thinking that was impressive spirituality. But Jesus' answer stunned everyone: effectively His reply was a way of saying "Every time." Jesus shows us another important aspect of putting relationships right when they have gone wrong in Matthew 18, which we will look at in Chapter 23.

To have to forgive a brother every time was hard enough, but Jesus made it even more difficult when He taught about love for our enemies in the Sermon on the Mount (Matthew 5:43–48). In effect, this is the same as "do to others as you would have them do to you" (Matthew 7:12). Roman soldiers were the most obvious enemy at the time. Palestine was occupied. Soldiers represented the power of the Empire, and to stay in control they had various unpleasant ways of treating ordinary people. So, it was revolutionary of Jesus to forbid violent overthrow of the enemy, let alone to teach about love of the enemy. They might treat you badly, but you must treat them as you would like to be treated.

How do we apply that in our context? Is there a colleague or a family member or someone else you know who is making life difficult for you? The spiritual dimension is to forgive and pray for them (and, if appropriate, to take authority over the demonic forces at work). The practical dimension is to treat them well, at least as well as you would like them to treat you. Their conscience might be brought to life by this, but even if not, we are called to overcome evil with good (Romans 12:19–21).

All this is impossible for us human beings on our own, but I am so glad that God does not leave us alone to follow Jesus. Instead, the Spirit is at work in us "to will and to work for his good pleasure," as Paul says in Philippians 2:13, bringing together the spiritual and practical dimensions.

20. Staying together

These days, we are accustomed to high rates of marriage failure — so much so that many people do not regard it as failure at all, simply recognising that people change. Sadly, it has been true in churches that relationships often fail and so, many churches split. It is as though the worldviews and values in society around us form our thinking and make us numb to the pain of relationships breaking down. Above all, we can grow numb to God's pain in seeing humans, who are made in His image with the ability to make choices, deliberately turning against His way of living.

God makes covenants — solemn and binding promises or agreements. His heart is that we should make covenants and keep them because of love: "until death parts us," not "until we find something more convenient or less challenging." His purpose ever since the Fall has been "to reconcile to himself all things [including all people], whether on earth or in heaven, by making peace through the blood of his cross" (Colossians 1:20).

So, it is hardly surprising that the New Testament teaches clearly that we need our minds and instincts re-programmed or re-formed, away from the values of society around us and into conformity with God's character. "Set your minds on things that are above," Paul urges the Colossians, "not on things that are on earth. For you have died and your life is hidden with Christ in God" (Colossians 3:2–3). This is only possible if we have surrendered to King Jesus, been born again and are living in Christ, so we have the Spirit at work in us (Romans 12:1–3).

When we live as part of the new creation, we can build relationships that last. Friendship grows in three levels or stages:

1.   When we start to get to know someone, we see one another in action. Our words and what we do give insight into what we are like and what matters to us. Often this is an exciting stage as we like what we see on the surface. But it is only on the surface.

2.   When we get to know one another better, we understand one another's character and personality. This is often a stage of disappointment. It is like seeing beneath the veneer of a fine-looking piece of furniture where it is chipped and finding it is not entirely solid wood after all, but more like chipboard. It might take some time to get to this stage. Romance or a common interest might keep a friendship going for a few years. However, this second stage is both dangerous and important: dangerous because we might be tempted to give up, and important because we can choose to push through to a deeper level of understanding

with a friend or to keep to a marriage covenant. If we make that choice, it leads to the third stage.

3.   When we decide to accept the other for who they are and choose to develop the friendship, we start to experience each other as the people we really are.

The first stage leads to the second, and the second to the third. This progression can be true of any relationship, but it matters most in two contexts: marriage and church.

If we are disciples, then God wants us to be like Him and stay committed to a marriage covenant. This is not the place to go into New Testament teaching on marriage and divorce, but Jesus made clear that a marriage covenant is important (Matthew 5:31–32 and Mark 10:2–12). There is a place for divorce if the other party is unfaithful, but there is always grace for those who stumble. There is a place for a fresh start, but if we are following Jesus, then He calls us to faithfulness and loyalty; and this includes commitment where we have made a lifelong promise. Paul took up Jesus' teaching about the reason for this: the two become one in God's eyes (Ephesians 5:25–33). He was teaching both about marriage relationships and the intimate relationship between Jesus and His Bride, the church.

The progression to the third stage matters also in the church because God's intention is that we should all be united.

Jesus' prayer in John 17 expresses what was most important to Him just hours before the crucifixion. "As you, Father, are in me and I am in you, may they also be in us...," He prayed, "...that they may become completely one" (John 17:21 and 23a). He went on to explain the purpose of this oneness: "so that the world may know that you have sent me and have loved them even as you have loved me" (John 17:23).

Unity of heart — being committed to one another despite our failings and with all our different personalities and gifts and callings — really matters to God. In fact, the purpose of ministries serving the church is so that *all* disciples will be equipped for service and building up the Body "until all of us come to the unity of the faith and of the knowledge of the Son of God, to maturity, to the measure of the full stature of Christ" (Ephesians 4:13).

God's purpose in making humans in the first place, and in salvation, is to bring us all together in Christ. Of course, many reject Him. But the church's calling is to give everyone the opportunity to respond to God and become disciples, to become part of the glorious, worldwide community that reaches towards knowing Christ and making Him known.

Unity with all God's people is important, living in a way that is loving and open to all who are in Christ. While this can seem a bit theoretical and remote, let us determine in our everyday lives to give expression to unity as we share lives with a community of disciples. It is worth the effort of forgiving and passing over offences. It is worth the effort of allowing the Spirit to join us with people who are not like us and whom we might not naturally like. It is worth the effort of loving one another.

There are many "one another" instructions in the New Testament which make a good Bible study with an online Bible concordance or search tool. But they can be summarised in three P's: *persevere* in commitment, *pray* for one another and *prefer* one another. Why would we do this? Because we love one another. Why do we love one another? Because it is the way we express our love for God in response to His amazing love for us.[14]

---

[14] John 13:34–35, as we saw in Chapter 17

Among the tribes: The wider family

21. Together apart: One universal church

So far, we have thought about how we as individuals respond to God's love and then find we are part of a family, the church. We have no option about being born into the family: as the early church leader and theologian Cyprian wrote, "He cannot have God as a father who has not the church for his mother."[15] We have looked at church mainly in terms of the fellow disciples we are in touch with and rooted together with. The local church might be a small group meeting informally or it might be a larger group made up of many small groups. But we know the names and faces of the people involved, and hopefully, we know and are known by some of them very well.

However, the church is bigger than the handful of disciples with whom we are building closely. In fact, it is made up of all who are *in Christ* or who have been born again by the Holy Spirit. It is not limited in geography or in time but includes all who have been born again, even if they describe it in different ways and worship in different ways from us.

---

[15] See *De Ecclesiae Catholicae Unitate* Section 6

The Nicene Creed is a foundational statement of faith produced in the fourth century and accepted by almost all Christian denominations or other movements. It includes a short sentence that may sound strange to us until we understand the technical language: "We believe in one holy catholic and apostolic church." In that short sentence are two words we need to understand to be able to grasp the meaning of this important statement of faith: catholic and apostolic.

Does the word 'catholic' here refer to the Roman Catholic Church? No, it is simply a word that the theologians used to mean universal. At the time of the Council of Nicaea in 325 AD, which produced the basic creed, and even the Council in 381 AD that added this statement and other material to it, it was just about possible to consider the Christian church as one universal church. It looked as though the church was united organisationally. But this was only if the small heretical or splinter groups were ignored.

The result of the Council was to crystallise some divisions between groups. These different groups seemed to worship the same Father through the same Christ by the same Spirit, often using similar patterns of prayer, but they expressed their teaching in different ways as the scholars tried to tie down the truth to precise, philosophical definitions.

As we saw in Chapter 13, however, the ultimate Truth is a Person, Jesus.

So, even at the time the Nicene Creed was adopted, it was hard to consider the church as one united organisation, and the very act of defining truth in words caused divisions. However, there is still this hope-filled declaration in the creed: that we believe in *one* universal church. Unity matters to God and to His people.

Unity does not mean being one organisation or institution, nor does it mean thinking the same about doctrines or trying to express them in the same words. Real unity does not even mean doing things the same and worshipping in the same ways, because God has created people with the ability to produce a beautiful diversity of languages and cultures. Unity means being of one heart and being single-minded (or intentional) about what really matters. We *preserve* the unity of the Spirit — we cannot create it, but we can preserve in the natural dimension what God has done in the spiritual dimension. We are part of one huge family of disciples, *one* universal church, whether we like how others do things or not.

Does the word 'apostolic' mean there has to be some kind of "apostolic succession" where we trace who laid hands on each senior overseer, back to one of the original Twelve Apostles who started this process? No, but it does mean that the church, if it is truly church in its nature, has to be based on the ministry of apostles. We will consider this in Chapter 24.

When Ezekiel saw a vision of the valley of dry bones, he was prompted by the Spirit to prophesy life and he saw the scattered bones come together as people, making up a vast multitude (Ezekiel 37:1–14). Yet the multitude was made up of people as the bones connected and sinews and flesh were formed. It is a prophetic picture delivered to the exiled Israelites of Ezekiel's day, who thought that God had completely abandoned His people and the promise of His presence being seen among human beings. It gave hope that God would one day raise up a multitude of people full of His life.

We are part of that multitude. But, like living stones in a building or parts of a human body, we each need to be linked closely together with the handful of people God has rooted us with. Ezekiel's vision speaks both of small groups and of the whole multitude of people. The small groups are like the individual bodies that are a picture of local churches or groups of disciples, where each member of the body is needed but contributes in different ways. The multitude is a picture or symbol of the one universal Body of the church, made up of all disciples of all time who are in Christ spiritually.

22. Together apart: One united church

We have seen that unity is God's intention for us as we learn to love one another in response to the love of God.[16] Unity is also important because it reflects and expresses the unity of the three Persons of the Godhead. It is not merely a desirable characteristic of the church, it is essential to the nature and work of the church.

This is explored further in Paul's letters, in which he gives some practical illustrations and teaching on the outworking of unity. Much of the emphasis of Paul's ministry was to achieve unity between Jewish and Gentile believers. Raising finance from Gentile churches to support the Jewish disciples in Jerusalem and the surrounding region was a major project. Perhaps he even saw it as a sign of his life's work. Also, it was the direct cause of his imprisonment in Jerusalem and the chain of events that led to his visit to Rome, in a way he had not expected when writing in Romans 1:10 of his longing to visit the church there. He was probably executed as an indirect result of wanting to deliver this support.

The contribution to the needs of Jewish believers was a sign of Paul's passionate concern for unity between Christians

---

[16] **See Chapter 17**

that comes across in almost all his letters. Paul was a Jewish follower of Jesus, looking for God's promises to Israel to be fulfilled in Christianity. His main ministry, however, was among Gentiles, and the particular revelation he seems to have received on his conversion was that the people of God are redefined in Christ to include Gentiles. All who put their trust in Christ are included in the new humanity, the new creation, and it is trust in Christ, or reliance on relationship with Him, that defines the boundaries, not observance of the Law.[17]

Paul's implicit theology is expressed particularly in Galatians (with a passionate plea to ignore the Judaisers who required observance of the Law), Romans (with a passionate plea for unity as part of the new creation and new people of God) and Ephesians (with a passionate plea for unity to express God's character, wisdom and power).

The letters to the Romans and Ephesians deal with other themes too, but unity is the overriding theme. For those who have been baptised and are therefore clothed with Christ, he asserts, "there is no longer Jew or Greek, there is no longer slave or free, there is no longer male or female; for all of you are one in Christ Jesus. And if you belong to Christ, then you are Abraham's offspring, heirs according to

---

[17] See, for example, the letter to the Galatians, especially 2:15–21 and 3:23–29

the promise" (Galatians 3:27–29). Inclusion is on the basis of being in Christ, and all other religious, economic or social divisions are obliterated. The church is therefore in a unique position as the expression in human form of the people of God, to whom the promises belong.

The implications are significant, including the following four points.

First, the church does not somehow replace the Jewish people (as many mediaeval and Reformation theologians taught), because in Christ we are Abraham's heirs.

Second, the Jewish people do not have a separate standing of their own in the covenant dealings of God with His people (as those following J.N. Darby and D.W. Moody have taught), because they are included in the people of God by virtue of new birth into Christ, not natural birth into an ethnic group or by observing the Mosaic Law.

Third, the Old Testament promises, which seem so concrete and specific to a certain ethnic group in a certain geography, have to be interpreted in a spiritual sense in the light of Jesus. Since the Cross, the Law is no longer the definition of the people of God. Rather, the determining factors are being in Christ and therefore being filled with the Spirit.

Fourth, the purpose of the church is no less than to express the character and wisdom of God, as Paul explains in

Ephesians 3 — it is to be an expression of all the fullness of God in human form. In other words, the church has an incarnational calling to continue what Jesus began. This is implicit in Acts 1:1–2 and Colossians 1:24 but is explicit in much of Jesus' teaching, such as Matthew 5:13–16 or His sending the disciples and the seventy out to continue His Luke 4:18–19 ministry in the villages.

Paul's vision of unity, and Christ's ministry of reconciliation to achieve it, are stated strongly and passionately throughout these epistles. However, there is a practical outworking of the huge vision. Each congregation needs to learn to welcome one another with love and respect despite their ethnic, social, economic and religious differences. There are times when this means welcoming people who are naturally considered dangerous enemies, perhaps part of a rival tribe or ethnic group. Unity is far more than just a general theory: its specific applications to our lives include welcoming enemies as well as handling differences of view over doctrine or what behaviour is acceptable.

There are many examples of former enemies being transformed by the power of the Spirit to be able to forgive and to build real friendship. As we have seen, forgiveness is a choice, not a feeling, and it is not just forgetting what happened. In fact, for people to process trauma well, they need to recognise what happened. Ideally, those on opposing sides will come together to tell the truth, recognise the facts, admit the wrongs and therefore be able to forgive and seek forgiveness. Only with these foundations can real understanding and friendship develop.

After the collapse of the apartheid system in South Africa, Archbishop Desmond Tutu and other Christian leaders were key to establishing the Truth and Reconciliation Commission. Perpetrators of violence were given an amnesty, free from prosecution for their crimes, if they would only testify about what they had done. At first it seemed unfair to the victims that their persecutors would be free from criminal sanctions. But as the hearings went on, often with gruesome details causing family and friends to shudder with horror as they learned what had really happened to loved ones, miracles happened. Perpetrators wept and asked for forgiveness. Victims wept and offered forgiveness. The truth came out into the open and people were set free in many different ways as a result.

My family have been privileged to meet a pioneer Christian leader from the mountainous Ayacucho region of Peru. She studied in the UK for two years and became a friend and part of our church. She told us of her grandfather, a pastor in an Andean village, being executed in front of his congregation by the Communist insurgent group Senderoso Luminoso during the long civil war. His widow was soon afterwards brutally raped by government forces, who suspected many of the villagers of sympathising with the insurgents, and thrown into an icy pool, left for dead. She survived, and she and her family members chose the way of Jesus, forgiving the wrongs and carrying on the work of preaching the gospel to all. In fact, one of our friend's uncles used to seek out Senderista guerrillas so he could preach about the Prince of Peace: miraculously, he was never killed in the attempts. Our friend determined to go back to live in the dangerous region to set up a clinic and join in the work of making disciples and planting churches.

Relationships in church are tested by offences and misunderstandings, as well as differences in how we worship and how we define our understanding of the truth in words. Yet, if victims of such evil crimes can extend forgiveness and be reconciled, surely we can forgive and be reconciled. If the Jewish and Gentile Christians of Paul's day could be united as a sign to the world of the amazing miracle of reconciliation achieved by Jesus at the Cross, then we can make unity our aim. It matters so much to God, so unity should matter to us.

23. Families, clans and tribes

There are different images in the New Testament to describe the church: a people, a holy nation, an army, a temple, a building, an olive tree, a vine, a bride, a body and a family. They all speak of being joined together and of some aspect of the purpose of the church.

A people or nation speaks of a large number joined together, perhaps a numberless multitude. The picture of an army suggests fighting spiritual battles in prayer. A temple points to our purpose as a dwelling place for God. An olive or vine speaks of connections and organic growth as we draw life from the root, Jesus Himself. The bride suggests intimacy with the Lord and the church being prepared for the consummation of the ages when Jesus will return. A body depends on all its members. The image of family is perhaps the most fundamental, as God reveals Himself as the Father, who made creation to be a beautiful expression of community. This community is achieved through Jesus, who made it possible for us to be born into the new creation by the Spirit.

How do we see this community coming into existence? How do we see these images working in practice in the different aspects of church? We have already noted the small, local aspect of church and the universal aspect, considering all Christians of all times and all geographies. But the different images suggest there may be more than just local and universal.

Maybe our idea of local church is not small enough in numbers and not big enough in vision for the depth of connections and local roots in a community. Perhaps our idea of the universal church is not adequate to encompass the rich diversity of styles and approaches while being united in heart. And there is room for other types of connection that link small, local churches together and give practical expression to the fact that each one is part of the universal church.

The Old Testament background gives some insight, as so often, in symbolic or picture form, into the New Testament realities. In Joshua 7:14–18, God instructs Joshua to present the whole people by tribes, from which He would choose one. Then from that one, the clans are presented and then the families. He could have simply pointed out which household within which family had sinned and caused the problems for the whole people, but God chose to select in this way to emphasise the way the holy nation was made up. How do we understand the different aspects of church?

A family is the local church. It might be a handful of people or it might be made up of a number of individuals and households or natural families. The family is where each disciple belongs, even though he or she did not choose to be born into that family. The local church is where we are joined by the Holy Spirit with the handful of fellow disciples who are the living stones we are being built with (or the parts of the Body we are closest to).

We are accustomed to thinking of a local church as a congregation meeting in a building, but in the early church (until the late third century) and in places where there is persecution, the normal gathering would have been, and is, in a home or other convenient place for a handful of brothers and sisters to meet. Often it was, and is, around a meal, which is the natural context for breaking bread together.

When Jesus referred to the church in Matthew 18:17, He was addressing a relatively small group of disciples, the ones who were following Him and with Him that day. The implication is that this miscellaneous group of misfits, some of them considered outcasts by religious people, was in effect Jesus' church family at the time. He is teaching them how to resolve misunderstandings and disputes between themselves, knowing that these will arise however small and committed the group of disciples. The first step is to speak truth in love and confront the person you think is in the wrong, but gently and with the aim of winning him or her back into loving fellowship. If that does not resolve it, and usually it will, then take one or two witnesses. Their job is not to add weight or to bully the other person but to check who is carrying a wrong attitude — a disagreement is less likely to descend into an argument if one or two other disciples are there as well. Only if this does not achieve reconciliation should the issue be brought to the church.

We think of family as the place everyone belongs, and of course we want to include people into this family fellowship. But there is a place for recognising where people count themselves out. The family is centred on Jesus, and it is relationship with Jesus that defines the family. So, if people do not want to live in love as part of the family, we have to recognise the true situation. Over the years, this has been abused or become a legal and bureaucratic process in some churches and has therefore been ignored in most. Acknowledging this withdrawal from fellowship is difficult and cumbersome if we consider church to be an organisation or legal entity. But it becomes real in the context of a small church family.

The point is not to follow a legal procedure but to recognise that someone has counted themselves out of the family by holding a wrong attitude (usually refusing to forgive or refusing to apologise). The issue is no longer the original offence or misunderstanding but the attitude of heart. Why? Because the purpose is to achieve reconciliation as part of the Kingdom coming: Jesus died and rose again to reconcile all people and all of creation (Colossians 1:20).

So, the basic unit of church is a family. We are born into a local family but can take ourselves out by wrong attitudes, acting as though we are not in the family but back in the world system. The church family is where we learn to be disciples, free from domination by the demonic powers of this present evil age. Our church family might be as small as a group of three or four, for example in a situation of intense persecution, or it may be larger in number, but the key is that it is small enough for real relationships and to share a meal together.

Each family in a traditional society belongs to a clan or larger unit, and this was also demonstrated by the Israelites in Joshua 7. We can think of this as a number of families or 'home churches' that are related by being in the same geographical area or by being established through the ministry of the same team of apostles and prophets. Or we can think of a clan as an apostolic family of churches or network, like All Nations, which enables local churches to co-operate and benefit from each other's resources (particular skills or strengths in certain areas as well as gifts and ministries). The difference between this sort of network and a traditional denomination is simply that it is based on relationship, not organisation. People and churches are joined together by relationships formed by the Spirit rather than membership or accepting the rules or constitution of the denomination.

The clans of Israel were each part of a tribe, and we can think of this as a group of clans. One example in our context is the All Nations Movement, which is a family of churches and whole networks. It is one of many apostolic families and movements. The tribes may look very different from each other as the various networks explore their own identities to fulfil their particular calling. Just as each family is different because of the individuals in it, so clans and tribes have distinctive characteristics. It takes all the tribes to make up the whole nation, the whole church or people of God.

24. Foundations

Whether we are thinking of a small local home church or of the whole nation, the church has a shape determined by its structure or foundations. We want to be linked by living relationships formed by the Spirit that reflect the life of the Spirit, but that is not an alternative to having some sort of structure. A body needs a skeleton and an olive tree is defined by its roots, trunk and branches; an army has divisions and ranks while a temple or other building has foundations. Even a natural family takes on the characteristics of the parents and is defined by the various relationships within it. In each case, a church needs some shape to enable the life of the Spirit to be established and visible to those around, not just to be experienced for a moment and then melt away.

The foundations of any building define its shape, size and ultimately its height. The image of foundations is one that Paul uses to explain how apostles and prophets contribute to the churches they serve. He begins at the end of Ephesians 2, after teaching on the unity of the church made up of Jews and Gentiles. Together, all God's people are "built upon the foundation of the apostles and prophets, with Christ Jesus himself as the chief cornerstone. In him the whole structure…grows into a holy temple in the Lord; in whom you also are built together spiritually into a dwelling place for God" (Ephesians 2:20–22).

Then, in Ephesians 3, Paul expresses the giddy heights of his vision for the church: the power to know the unknowable love of Christ and be filled with all the fullness of God (i.e. hosting God on earth). Chapter 4 of Ephesians earths us again. Paul is a prisoner, waiting for the Kingdom that has come in part to be fully revealed in future. He calls his readers to live well, which means to live like Jesus in practice, with humility, gentleness, patience and love. These are not just instructions, like a new version of the Law, they are prophetic descriptions of what the future will be like. They help us take hold of the future and bring it into the present by the power of the Spirit. In our own strength it would be impossible, but this is a supernatural process of praying "Your Kingdom come" and living accordingly.

Paul teaches that we are to make "every effort to maintain the unity of the Spirit in the bond of peace" (Ephesians 4:3) because there is one Body. This leads him to thinking about the ministries the risen Christ has given to the church. The purpose of the ministries is clear and must be emphasised: "to equip the saints for the work of ministry, for building up the Body of Christ, until all of us come to the unity of the faith and of the knowledge of the Son of God, to maturity, to the measure of the full stature of Christ"

(Ephesians 4:12–13). Because there is one Body, as Paul has just explained in Ephesians 4:1–5, these ministries are needed to bring the church into unity and maturity. Their role will not be complete until the end, the Second Coming of Christ.

In Western culture, when we think of the roles people fulfil, our minds are conditioned to think of their function and where they fit into an organisational structure: "What is the role?" is a question that leads very quickly to "What is their position and authority?" In the New Testament, however, the emphasis is on "What do they bring to the church?"

The ministries listed in Ephesians 4:11 are not about structure or hierarchy: the emphasis is on what grace the ministries bring. Their function is to equip *all* the saints for the work of ministry and building up the Body, not to be the main ministers. Have we misinterpreted the essential nature of these different gifts? Key ministers or leaders are not superheroes but in fact suffer more than others (Paul explains this in the extended defence of his ministry in 2 Corinthians 10–12). Each member of the Body is involved in service within the church and outside into the communities around. The primary purpose of these ministries is to enable each member of the Body to function. This means each member will play their part in fulfilling the

Great Commission to make disciples as they go about the daily business of life.

An apostle is literally "one sent" and the word was used in New Testament times of an ambassador or messenger. An apostle is sent out with a *particular* message that God intends for the season and a specific purpose. Apostles and prophets together provide a foundation for the churches in their sphere of ministry: the relational connection is a security and foundation (Ephesians 2:20). Their scope is trans-local.

We need to address the apparent contradiction in 1 Corinthians 3:11. No foundation can be laid except Christ, yet apostles and prophets are foundational. Ephesians 2 makes clear that Jesus is the cornerstone, which in New Testament times would be the first foundation stone to be positioned and would define the alignment and often even the size of the house to be built. Then all the other living stones are positioned and joined to Christ.

When apostles and prophets provide a foundation to a particular church in various ways (by their example, making connections with other members of the Body, teaching and working signs and wonders), they are bringing to earth the foundation laid in heaven. They are connecting the church to Jesus Himself. So, Paul could speak of Christ being formed in the believers for whom he was responsible as a result of his ministry and that of others in his apostolic sphere.

Such a building can grow and develop — in fact, the building analogy breaks down at the point we recognise that the foundational ministries themselves grow in grace and develop. The scope of Paul's ministry grew over time as he made disciples, planted churches and served as a father to those churches planted out of them. This concept of foundation is still helpful, though. It implies definition, shape and scope but also the expectation of expansion as each of the saints plays their part together.

Apostles help bring good order and the spiritual wisdom to appoint leaders in churches, so the message can be embodied and carried out to its fullest extent.

Prophets are those who have particular gifts and a calling to see more of what God is doing and to point the way forward. Without other ministry gifts in close team connection, they can feel so far ahead that they are uncomfortable in the setting they find themselves, but together they can trust other, more pastoral ministries to share the word in ways that people can apply.

Other ministry gifts are essential in the church too. Evangelists might take the lead in proclaiming the gospel, but their role is also to equip all the disciples to embody and to explain the good news of Jesus. Evangelists are not only those who announce the gospel but — according to the norms in the book of Acts — do so in a context of signs and wonders.

The ministries of teaching and shepherding overlap and can be seen as one or two separate ministries. It is not crucial to decide whether there are four or five ministry gifts to the church in Ephesians 4:11 because shepherds and teachers have a similar role of modelling truth — incarnating truth in human lives — and explaining truth by reference to the scriptures so that people encounter the Spirit and are changed into the likeness of Jesus. Shepherds in the Middle East lead from the front, not from behind, and there are indications in the New Testament that the roles of shepherds and teachers involve challenging and not just encouraging. For example, the purpose of scripture as revealed by Paul in 2 Timothy 3:16 is "for teaching, for reproof, for correction and for training," so we may take it that at least half of the ministry involves challenging concepts and behaviours that reveal character issues.

However, in each case, the aim is not to do all the work of ministry but to provide an example and inspiration and to equip, or facilitate or enable, all the disciples to make disciples.

25. Apostolic teams and the message they bring

It is important for the Ephesians 4:11 ministry gifts to work together in teams. This is not just because teamwork is efficient and effective, but also because it reflects the nature of God: one God in three Persons, all of whom are involved in all that God does. An apostle carries a particular message for the context, for a particular purpose or maybe for a whole season. However, the message is not disembodied words. It cannot be expressed just by preaching and teaching but needs to be demonstrated in the lives of the apostle and the team of ministries working together with the apostle, through supernatural signs and wonders and through being examples of holiness. It seems Paul took his role of being an example so seriously he saw it as imparting himself to the churches (2 Corinthians 12:12; 1 Thessalonians 2:8 and 4:1–2). In his epistles, Paul uses several different descriptions of his team members, including:

- Prophet (Acts 13:1; 15:32)

- Evangelist (2 Timothy 4:5)

- Shepherd (1 Corinthians 9:7)

- Teacher (Acts 13:1)

- Servant (helper) (1 Corinthians 4:1)

The diversity of ministries among his team suggests that an apostolic team should not be limited to apostles. The full range of ministries referred to in Ephesians 4:11 are included. Their different approaches are all needed to embody and express the key message that the apostle carries.

Teamwork can be messy, particularly if there are strong characters and different gifts and therefore different concerns. But the importance of unity in diversity is recognised not only in theological discussions but in management science and related disciplines. There is much research suggesting that leaders need humanity and humility to lead a team well. Although this not universally accepted, I would endorse it strongly from my experience in business and in church. One aspect of this is that great leaders can draw out the best ideas through asking questions rather than giving input. Jesus is presented in the Gospels as combining authority and humility, teaching by example and by dialogue. So, an apostle is a leader but should lead in a Christlike way, as a servant. Paul even describes apostles like him as being "last of all, as though sentenced to death" (1 Corinthians 4:9).

Other descriptions used by Paul of his team members are also revealing:

- Brother (Acts 22:5; Romans 16:23)

- Child (1 Timothy 1:2)

- Slave or fellow slave (Philippians 1:1)

- Partner (2 Corinthians 8:23)

- Fellow soldier (Philippians 2:25)

- Fellow worker (Romans 16:3; 9 and 21)

These descriptions and the way he wrote to Timothy and Titus seem to reveal a close relationship that is far beyond a typical working relationship. There is a warmth of affection and depth of relationship implicit in the words Paul chose to use. In fulfilling his calling and leading his team, he was not like a business leader but a father.

In fact, Paul was conscious that his role in relation to the churches in his sphere of ministry was to be a father. In 1 Corinthians 4:14–17, we have a glimpse of what this meant. He had to warn the Corinthians about their divisions, shown in the way they were choosing to listen only to certain favourite ministers. He reminds them that he is their father in the gospel and appeals to them to imitate his lifestyle and behaviour. Paul explains he sent Timothy to be an example of his own ways: he had discipled Timothy, who had received and acted on Paul's example and training. So, in seeing Timothy, they would see a reminder of

Paul's ways "as I teach them everywhere in every church" (1 Corinthians 4:17).

This gives more insight into what is meant by "the apostles' teaching" in Acts 2:42 and generally in the New Testament. It is not theoretical but embodied. It is not just ideas, but words and ideas rooted in real character and lifestyle. It is not just good advice on how to live well but a dynamic impartation of spiritual life. Speaking "in the Spirit" does not mean sounding weird or feeling particularly inspired but speaking in a way that carries spiritual authority so that lives change as a result. This is how apostles lay foundations in churches.

In 1 Corinthians 2:12–13, Paul explains that the Holy Spirit enabled him to understand the gifts placed in him and inspired his teaching. The apostles and the other ministries in their teams are "interpreting spiritual things to those who are spiritual" (1 Corinthians 2:13). Some apostles may express the message they carry as a more prophetic message and others may sound like Bible teachers as they speak. The first group may have more emphasis in their ministry on seeing and giving direction, and the latter more on setting things in order.

The team of apostles, prophets, evangelists, shepherds and teachers that a particular apostle leads will naturally be shaped by the same message. Some team members may have grown to maturity because of the leader, like Timothy, so it is natural they will carry the same emphasis and minister from that same revelation. Others may have been attracted to the leader's ministry because the message resonates with them; it was the rallying point that prompted them to come close, and as they did so, they recognised the joining of heart that the Holy Spirit had made. Of course, there is no direct description of this in the New Testament, but it has been the experience of the All Nations Movement leadership team or apostolic team. With the benefit of that experience, we can read Acts and the epistles and see successful teamwork is implied in various places.

The process of reading and understanding scripture demonstrates why we need the whole church and the revelation that God gives to different teams, streams and denominations. Or, to use the language we prefer in All Nations, we need to hear the voices of people from across the whole "nation" — the whole people of God of all time and all geographies — not just our own tribe or clan. There is no problem with each clan having its own distinctive character and flavour, each apostolic team carrying its particular emphasis in the message it brings, provided we all remain open to further revelation from the Spirit communicated through other clans and tribes.

John Robinson, the pastor to the Pilgrim fathers, spoke of this openness in a sermon preached in 1620 before they embarked on the *Mayflower*:

> I charge you before God…that you follow me no further than you have seen me follow the Lord Jesus Christ. If God reveals anything to you by any other instrument of His, be as ready to receive it as you were to receive any truth by my ministry, for I am verily persuaded *the Lord hath more truth yet to break forth out of His Holy Word* [emphasis by author].

26. Belonging: In the world but not of the world

"You're too heavenly minded to be any earthly use" is the complaint of an activist frustrated by emphasis on devotional life — encountering God in scripture and in prayer. The accusation is like Martha's frustration with Mary for not helping with hospitality for Jesus and His disciples.

The story is told in Luke 10:38–42. Perhaps Martha was shocked mainly by the fact that Mary wanted to learn as a disciple, which in their culture was a privilege for men and boys only while the women focused more on work. But she was certainly frustrated, and many readers take this as a simple choice: either work or be devoted. The assumption is that you can only do one or the other, and to Jesus being devoted is the "better part" or best choice. In fact, a literal translation is "the good portion," which to Jews of Jesus' day would have been instantly recognised as referring to the scriptures. Mary had chosen to hear Jesus recite and teach on the scriptures. It was not an either/or choice. No doubt, Mary helped and served wholeheartedly in practical ways. We do not know the details, but perhaps Martha could have chosen the same and then enlisted Mary's help with all the preparations. What matters is that we do not have to choose either devotion or action: both are needed.

In John's Gospel, there is much emphasis on devotion. "Abide in Me as I abide in you" is a significant theme. Yet it is not an introverted or self-serving contemplation or devotional time. In John 15:5, Jesus links abiding, or remaining or resting in Him, with bearing fruit, and in John 15:7, Jesus makes clear that "If you abide in me and my words abide in you, ask for whatever you wish and it will be done for you." Fruit comes naturally and organically, but we do not simply spend time in devotions and then hope to see fruit come without any further co-operation on our part. Instead, we pray as we act and we act prayerfully, noticing what Father God is doing around us so we can be fruitful in doing it with Him.

One theologian describes John's Gospel as a "missional gospel with a missional spirituality...a spirituality of participation in the very life and life-giving mission of God, by which Jesus' disciples demonstrate their likeness to God and become more and more like God."[18] Abiding is not just a passive contemplation or devotional time but a constant attitude of heart that bears fruit as we speak and act as well as pray.

We see this too in 2 Peter 1, where Peter writes that "His divine power has given us everything needed for life

---

[18] See Gorman *Abide and Go: Missional Theosis in the Gospel of John* p. xvii. The title sums up the message!

and godliness," (verse 3). Through His promises we may "become participants of the divine nature" (verse 4). It is His power and promises that enable us to change and become more like Him in our behaviour. Then, in verses 6–8, Peter urges us to make efforts. There is work for us to do as we make godly choices and act in accordance with nature. It is still His power at work in us but we have to choose to live by His power.

Another theologian writes of the effect of prayer and contemplation:

> When he [any Christian, male or female] emerges from prayer, he is not blinded by yonder glory, unable to come to grips with the world here below, and yearning to retire to contemplation's blissful meadows; he appears as someone *sent*, who has received in contemplation (without being aware of it) all the equipment he needs for his Christian mission: the authority, the abilities and the taste for it.[19]

The purpose, then, of prayer and scripture is not to grow holy in isolation. In fact, it is impossible. Character is only tested in relationships. As John Wesley wrote, "The gospel of Christ knows of no religion, but social; no holiness but

---

[19] See Urs von Balthasar *Prayer* p. 139

social holiness. Faith working by love is the length and breadth and depth and height of Christian perfection."[20] Besides, holiness is to be shared so that others can encounter God and be changed to become more like Him. Jesus' prayer in John 17 gives insight into how our spirituality or devotional life affects the world around us. It will be helpful to read John 17 before going on and to refer to it in the rest of this chapter as we work through it.

We can see from some important little words like "from," "in," "into," "of" and "out of" how we relate with the world around us. Firstly, though, we need to be clear about the two principal ways the New Testament uses the word "world." One meaning is simply the creation, the physical world around us. The other is more symbolic or general and refers to the world system, or humanity acting in independence from God. The world as creation is neutral and is capable of being really good (as God intended when He made it) or dangerous (when events like earthquakes or storms occur). The world as humanity acting independently of God is in rebellion against Him and is dominated by evil, demonic powers. That is why Paul wrote in Ephesians 2:1–3 that we were spiritually dead when we followed the course of this world and followed "the ruler of the power of the air." From a human point of view, it might seem that

---

[20] See John Wesley *Hymns and Sacred Poems (1739 edition)* **Preface**

we were only living by our human abilities, according to what we see and feel and think, but that is what Paul describes as living "in the flesh," and the *spiritual* reality is that by doing so we are being led by demonic powers. The good news, of course, is that God brought us to life spiritually because of Jesus and delivered us from the demonic powers (Ephesians 2:4–9; Galatians 1:3–4).

Now we can work through Jesus' prayer (John 17):

Verse 6

> They (the disciples) were "*from* the world." They and we are all subject to sin and death, dominated by demonic powers and in rebellion against God. This is our starting point.

Verse 11

> "I (Jesus) am no longer *in* the world but they are *in* the world." Jesus is looking ahead a day or so, to when the disciples will be without Him (though He had already promised that the Spirit will come upon them in John 14, which in the long term is actually better for them and us).

Verse 13

> "I (Jesus) speak…*in* the world" (now).

Verse 14

> "They do not belong *in* the world" (KJV: "they are not *of* the world") just as Jesus Himself does not belong to

the world. When we are born again into new life, we are in Christ, as we have seen, and part of a new creation. We are free from the demonic powers because of Jesus' death and resurrection. We share in His eternal life now and therefore need not fear death because eternal life will last forever. We take on the family likeness, becoming more like Jesus and living according to the leading of the Spirit who enables us to want what is right and to do it (Philippians 2:13). This has enormous implications: we are called to live as children of God, and Jesus painted a picture of what this looks like in the Sermon on the Mount (Matthew 5–7). It is radically different from the lifestyle of those around us because we have a different life source, and that brings on us the hatred of the demonic powers at work in many of the people around us.

Verse 15

"I (Jesus) am not asking you to take them *out of* the world but to protect them." We need God's protection and can expect complete protection spiritually, even though we may well suffer physically and emotionally and mentally because the Kingdom is both here among us and not yet here, as we saw in Chapter 10.

Verse 16

"They do not belong *in* the world just as I (Jesus) do not."

Verse 18

"As You (God) have sent Me (Jesus) *into* the world, so I (Jesus) have sent them *into* the world." We are in Christ and identify with Him. We carry on His mission, which is why He promised we would do even greater things than He could as an individual.

Verses 20 to 23

Finally, we read how that mission will be achieved: by the presence of God among us shown in practice by our love and unity. When people around sense God's glory, the weighty presence of God, and see supernatural signs of it, they will trust Jesus too. The greatest and most important sign of God's presence is our unity. "The glory you have given me I have given them, so that they may be one, as we are one...so that the world may know..."

We belong in the world because we are part of the natural creation but, more importantly, we belong spiritually to the new creation coming down from heaven to earth, so we do not belong to the world system. In fact, we provoke it by seeking the presence of God as we make godly choices to live according to what we hear and see in Him.

27. Learning from the past

What can we learn from history about being in the world but not of it, citizens of heaven and citizens of the nation or city where we live at the same time?

When Paul wrote the letter to the Philippians, he was chained to a Roman soldier. As a Roman citizen, he had appealed to Caesar's court and was waiting for years for his trial. He had plenty of time to ponder what it means to be a good citizen, and this comes out in the letter.

The early church had to face the question of how Christians relate with the earthly powers. Jesus had clearly demonstrated that he had not come to support any of the strong parties in contemporary Jewish society. He had not aligned with the Pharisees, who tried to retreat from the world into a religious space where they could fulfil the Law and pray. Nor did He agree with the Essenes who tried to retreat from the world altogether. He refused the option of the Zealots: violent resistance to the Roman occupiers. And He opposed the remaining option of the Sadducees and Herodians, which was collaboration with the Roman occupiers to maintain what political power they could. It was the High Priest and Sadducees who arranged for the crucifixion.

Ever since, the relationship between the church and the government has been a difficult one to work out. At the risk of over-simplifying, there are three main approaches in church history.

One is that "government is evil." When persecuted by the Roman state, it was easy for Christians in New Testament times to reject all human government. Some were so glad to be free as Christians that they were in danger of scorning authority and bringing the gospel into disrepute! So, Paul and Peter both instructed the church to respect human leaders (Romans 13; Peter 2:13–17, though these passages are not the whole story in the New Testament on how we relate with the state).

Another is that "government is how to get things done so we need to influence it." This seems to be a common approach among Christians in the USA today, many of whom will tolerate bad behaviour or extreme views from the President as long as legislation favouring certain causes can be passed. This was the approach taken by much of the church in the century after the Roman Emperor Constantine became a Christian. Tragically, during the fourth century Christians went from being persecuted to being persecutors. The church became polluted by power and overwhelmed by worldliness. We face the same danger today if we rely on human government to bring in the Kingdom of God.

The best approach, however, is that "government can be made better" through the prayer and witness of the church. I believe this is Jesus' approach: He lived free from control by the earthly or demonic powers so His presence would bring the Kingdom of God. It is a more difficult path to follow. In Philippians 1:27–2:18, Paul urges the church to live as good citizens among the people around them.[21] The famous passage in Philippians 2:6–11 was probably an early hymn but certainly expresses clearly Jesus' way of leading by being a servant, of exercising authority by seeming to give it all away.

Philippians 2:6–11 is not just a devotional passage and is certainly not limited to behaviour in church, but Paul is using this hymn to show how Christians should behave in public, how we can be good citizens of the nation or city we live in. While the Romans valued strength, Christians need to display the apparent weakness and humility of Jesus. It is a radical, revolutionary gospel message that in weakness we are truly strong.

---

[21] **Philippians 1:27 is translated as "live your life in a manner worthy..."**
(NASB) or "let your manner of life be worthy..." (ESV) but more
literally is "live as citizens in a manner worthy..."

Church history is filled with many inspiring examples but also many warnings of how not to behave. The sudden change from being persecuted to being honoured after Constantine's conversion in 312 AD was too good an opportunity to miss. Almost by accident, and with noble intentions, the church became closely linked with the Roman state. This made life difficult for the many Christians in the areas east of Jerusalem, who continued to be a tolerated or even persecuted minority (except in what became the origin of Armenia). They were often treated with suspicion as Roman sympathisers, especially when there was war.

Numbers in churches increased dramatically and standards of spirituality, holiness and commitment declined. There were no more martyrs to inspire and to whom people would look up to as examples of faith, but their place was taken by those who adopted a different sort of martyrdom: an ascetic lifestyle seeking depths of spirituality, holiness and commitment.

The first hermits lived in the desert but usually in informal communities and with some communal prayer and breaking bread. The first organised monastic community was established in Egypt in about 320 AD. Its founder, Pachomius, established a rule that prevented extremism and set the direction for monastic practice ever since.

There were regular meals and regular times of worship; his communities were self-supporting through working in various industries such as weaving mats or growing produce for sale; wealth and property belonged to the community. There was a probation period during which parts of the Bible were memorised, and if the probationers could not read, they were taught.

Monasticism spread and was a renewal movement within an increasingly lax church, which had come under the influence of the Roman Emperors and aristocrats, some of whom were appointed as bishops even though only recently converted. Basil of Caesarea established monasteries in Asia Minor, following the style of those influenced by Pachomius. He was both a hermit and a bishop (appointed on merit) and established a rule that still governs Greek Orthodox monasteries today. Basil explained two important reasons for communal life; first, that it is the context for expressing love of others and second, that it allows for mutual accountability.

The Syriac and Nestorian churches evangelised to the east, outside the Eastern Roman Empire (otherwise known as the Byzantine Empire) as far as South India and the central regions of China. The monastic rules were a little different but followed the same basic pattern. In the Western church, the rule established by Benedict at Monte Cassino in Italy became something of a standard. In each case the vows made could be summarised in renouncing the world and entering a life of prayer, study, work and service. But even in what looks like an escape from the world, there was a very strong emphasis throughout on serving the local cities and towns, especially the poor or the sick.

The vows or promises required by Benedict's rule are significant: "He who is to be received shall make a promise before all in the oratory of his stability and of the reformation of his life and of obedience."[22] This is sometimes expressed as vows of conversion (continuing reformation of character and dependence on God), stability and obedience. The promise of stability usually meant remaining in the monastery which the novice enters, and there were rules about a monk reporting to a senior monk or the abbot all that happened in any excursion outside. In the East and in Britain, however, there was some flexibility about movement, so the monastery provided the security of a home base, a community where the monk always belonged, rather than preventing travel. Obedience can be characterised as openness and accountability to the abbot or another senior monk or any other confessor: at worst it could

---

[22] See Benedict *The Rule of St. Benedict* Chapter 58

be abusive and hierarchical, but at best it would be a liberating mutual accountability.

The history of monasticism — like church history generally — is complex and varied but there are some common themes. There are two key learning points from the past as we seek to develop local church communities that are missional and look to the future. First, the value of keeping communities small, and second, the significance of making a promise of stability or rootedness. Communities of Christians committed to God and to one another are places of prayer, equipping and sending, bases for making disciples and planting new communities of disciples.

28. Citizens of heaven belonging to our neighbours on earth, part 1

The word 'alien' may bring up different pictures for us. For me, growing up in the 1960s on a limited diet of TV programmes and films, aliens meant imaginary creatures from other planets. There were Martians with aerials instead of ears and the strange creations seen on Dr Who and Star Trek. They look rather pathetic nowadays to youngsters used to digital imagery, but they were our imaginary aliens.

Or we might think of alien customs or ideas, things that we do not share. Some might think of aliens as foreign nationals, people who do not share the nationality of the country. It sounds a cold and exclusive way of speaking about people but, in many countries, it is the legally correct way of describing people who are of a different nationality.

In 1 Peter 2:11, we Christians are described as "aliens and strangers" (NASB), or "foreigners and exiles" (NIV) or "strangers and pilgrims" (KJV) — there are many different ways of translating the words, but the idea is that we are here but do not belong here. We might be good citizens of the UK or law-abiding visitors, but the truth is that as Christians we have a higher loyalty than nationality, a closer bond between us than the bond of sharing citizenship with others.

Paul makes this clear in Philippians 3:20: "our citizenship is in heaven."

Does that mean we are just passing through and should make no attachments with the people around us? No — we are not called to hide away from the people around us. We still live in the world, but Jesus prayed in John 17 that we will be kept from the evil one and that we will be made holy, which means "separated for God."

The separation is something that happens in our hearts, not in keeping away from people. In fact, Jesus specifically commissions us to get our hands dirty, to be among people who need help, who need Him. Holiness is not keeping away from certain things. Holiness is living wholeheartedly — literally from a heart made whole by God's grace — on the basis of our new citizenship being more important than any natural citizenship or other tie.

Holy people should really be more peaceful, more fun-loving, more generous and more self-sacrificial than others as they become more like Jesus, the only truly perfect human. Above all, they are Spirit-filled people, living in the natural world with supernatural power. No wonder Peter describes Christians as aliens.

Writing about 130 AD, an unknown Christian expresses this well in the Epistle to Diognetus.[23] It was probably written to someone who was being taught the faith and discipled as preparation for baptism. What he wrote still has a contemporary ring to it today:

> Christians are indistinguishable from others either by nationality, language or customs. They do not inhabit separate cities of their own, or speak a strange dialect, or follow some outlandish way of life…With regard to dress, food and manner of life in general, they follow the customs of whatever city they happen to be living in, whether it is Greek or foreign.
>
> And yet there is something extraordinary about their lives. They live in their own countries as though they were only passing through. They play their full role as citizens, but labor under all the disabilities of aliens. Any country can be their homeland, but for them their homeland, wherever it may be, is a foreign country.…

---

[23] **Available online in various sites and translations, such as http://www.earlychristianwritings.com/text/diognetus-lightfoot.html or https://files.romanroadsstatic.com/materials/romans/early-christianity/DiognetusV1-0.pdf**

They live in the flesh, but they are not governed by the desires of the flesh. They pass their days upon earth, but they are citizens of heaven. Obedient to the laws, they yet live on a level that transcends the law. Christians love all men, but all men persecute them...

To speak in general terms, we may say that the Christian is to the world what the soul is to the body. As the soul is present in every part of the body, while remaining distinct from it, so Christians are found in all the cities of the world, but cannot be identified with the world. As the visible body contains the invisible soul, so Christians are seen living in the world, but their spiritual life remains unseen.

At that time, the church was persecuted and a relatively small minority, but Christians were motivated by love to care for those around them. Plague was common and so was the practice of abandoning unwanted babies, especially girls. But Christians stood out as different; they were known for caring for the victims and adopting unwanted babies (which seems to me to be a better approach for the church to take than campaigning for or against particular abortion laws).

Some years after the letter to Diognetus was written, and again in the following century, there were major plagues that affected most of the Roman Empire. While others escaped to fresh air in the countryside, Christians were notable for staying in the cities so they could care for the sick and dying and deal with burying the dead. Many died as a result but were glad to serve for the sake of love.

This is how disciples behave when following Jesus. Following Jesus is not just a matter of personal behaviour but also of being missional, reaching out to the people around to continue Jesus' mission. And being witnesses includes not just words but miracles and the hard work of welcoming strangers, loving enemies and caring for all who are in need. As we participate in His life, we become agents of the coming Kingdom and do what Jesus did. That is a simple definition of mission, but in the next chapter we will think some more about mission.

29. Citizens of heaven belonging to our neighbours on earth, part 2

There are many definitions or understandings of mission, ranging from a typical dictionary definition of "a journey with a purpose" to complex theological constructs. I believe a concept of mission as discipleship is the most fruitful understanding of mission inspired by the Holy Spirit.

The starting point is the Great Commission, which the four Gospel writers recorded with different emphases:

- **Matthew's** version of Jesus' commission is the broadest: to make disciples (Matthew 28:18–20).

- **Mark** places more emphasis on disciple-making through miraculous signs (Mark 16:15–18).

- **Luke's** main focus is on awaiting the coming of the Spirit; only by the Spirit's power can we be witnesses and so make disciples (Luke 24:49; Acts 1:4–8).

- **John** too makes much of the Spirit, but in Jesus' breathing on the disciples rather than awaiting Pentecost (John 20:22–23). Another expression of the Commission in John emphasises being sent to bear fruit that will last. This is John 15:16, which is not generally recognised as a version of the Great Commission, but it seems to capture an important element of it: fruit.

The ultimate fruit is in the form of disciples who themselves reproduce. I suggest these are merely different perspectives on the same commission.

If we are truly people of the Spirit, then we will reproduce ourselves as we go into the world. The miraculous signs, the teaching and being witnesses are all part of our prime calling as church: making disciples. All the things we do can be summed up as "Words, Works and Wonders."

However, let's not fall into the trap of confining mission to "Words, Works and Wonders" or any other definition or model. If we do, it is quite likely we have missed the real point. When the eternal Word, the "eternally begotten" Son, was born as a human, Jesus was entering a hostile culture. God did not communicate remotely from afar but chose to humble Himself, become weak and vulnerable and ultimately to submit to torture and death. Incarnation is a radical and disturbing concept. Even using the theological term Incarnation can diminish our appreciation of just how radical it is.

What does this mean for us as we seek to reach out to those around us? Simply that if we are following Jesus, we will reach out in the same way He did. If we embrace 'incarnational mission' in the way Jesus did, it will have huge impact. Reaching the world means expressing the gospel in ways that are relevant for each people group. A people group is usually understood as a community defined by a shared language and culture. So, incarnational mission means living among a people group as a servant, adopting their lifestyle (except where something offends one's conscience as a Christian). It means voluntarily accepting limitations and letting go of the privileges of belonging to our own context and culture. It means looking and sounding very much like the host culture, except that the Christian displays the character of Jesus.

Perhaps it is impossible to become entirely like those born into a certain people group, but we can identify with them. A friend who led a small team planting a church in East London moved into an area with many needy people, an area of "multiple deprivation." A neighbour said "We will give you 12 months. Do-gooders come here and say they want to make a difference. Hah. Then they leave!" After he and his wife and young children had lived there three years and persevered in listening well and caring for people, many of the local people started to show interest in what they were doing, and the church started to grow as neighbours began to follow Jesus.

We do not just identify with the host culture but also bring a challenge, a call to live differently. Mary Thiessen was raised on a farm in the Canadian prairies but felt God's call to an inner-city mission serving poor Latinos in downtown

Los Angeles. The physical contrast could not have been greater: no space, lots of noise and bustle, people crowded together in the streets and in tenement blocks. Often a whole family would have to share a room with inadequate facilities. She learned Spanish but felt increasingly frustrated as she tried and failed to serve in various projects as her colleagues in the mission organisation were doing. She kept asking God what she could do. Breakthrough came when she realised that living in a crowded space herself and visiting people to care for them was only part of her life there. It gave her credibility with those around her, but she needed to bring her own rich experience of family life. Remembering the precious times of conversation and prayer around the table at home, she found she could invite people to share a meal, including sharing in the preparation so they felt part of the family. Mary brought the gift of being herself. She was not good at working in projects, but she was extremely good at building family relationships over the table. It changed the lives of many in that community.

Sometimes incarnational mission is across major language and cultural boundaries. When Hudson Taylor lived in China, he ate and dressed like a Chinese man. Of course, he remained a Victorian Englishman, but the simple ways he identified with the local people earned him the right to speak about "the strange Western religion" without it being rejected as just for the Westerners. The way Jesus called His disciples (John 1:39 and 43) suggests that once we have gained the right to speak and the attention of the host community, incarnational mission can be summed up in two statements: "come and see" and "come follow me."

To some extent we cross cultures whenever we move into a different community. Language and broad cultural features can be the same, but we need to listen and observe carefully. We have to be prepared to learn if we truly want to come alongside a new community. When Catherine and I moved with our young children from a prosperous suburb, with a higher proportion than most of professional people, to a former mining town, with a higher proportion than most of unemployed people, we had much to learn about the lifestyle of people very different from our own. We were young and inexperienced. But over the years and many cups of tea we began to appreciate our neighbours' perspectives and had a glimpse of their worldviews. Different priorities concerning time, education or money need to be respected. We tried to be sensitive and to listen well as we sought to understand this new environment spiritually, psychologically, socially, historically and geographically.

The key is to be ourselves. When we are at peace with our own identity we can be loving and teachable, prepared to enter into some of the same activities. On one occasion, that meant the two of us playing bingo in the Miners' Welfare because the caller's wife wanted to join the church and this was the only place where we could meet with her husband. The conversation opened the door to meaningful relationship with three generations of a key family.

Incarnational mission looks different in each community or people group, but we start with humility, coming alongside to discover the needs of the community and serving. We work *with*, not *for* the marginalised and poor as we seek to show God's love. Our lifestyle must display Jesus' character, living supernaturally, trusting God and expecting miracles. Of course, that may challenge the expectations of the people around us and even provoke a hostile reaction. Living like Jesus is costly because the key is loving people. But Jesus embraced the Cross and invites us to take up our cross and follow Him. Are we willing to follow?

30. Belonging: Purpose

We have looked at God's heart for each of us to be at home in Him and our responses as individuals (repent and be baptised) which include us in God's family. We have also looked at what the church is and what it looks like, including how the local, trans-local and universal church interlink. But what is the end goal? What is church really for?

Every person and every organisation has an inbuilt, natural instinct for self-preservation. It is as though we are designed to grow stronger and to grow ever more mature. This is a natural process and part of the creation: when God made plants, animals and people, He made us to be fruitful and to fill the earth and steward it well.

Of course, we live in a fallen world, a world where sin has spoilt the Creator's original design. Even though there are many signs of the image of God in all humans, and of the beauty and intricacy of creation in all creatures and things, the instinct for growth has been perverted into a desire to grow at the expense of others. Jesus demonstrated God's true heart and intention — pure love — when He came as a servant and humbled Himself (Philippians 2:5–11).

So, we can see the goal of the church is to reflect Jesus' character and to serve people in "Words, Works and

Wonders." But as it does so, should the church simply grow more mature, stronger and larger? Is there more? I believe there is and that Paul's letters show he was gripped by a cosmic vision for what the church would be and become.

To discover the purpose of the church, we have to step back into the Old Testament. This is because the purpose of the whole people of God has been consistent throughout salvation history, even though the Cross has revolutionised who is included in God's people and how we achieve His purposes. God's original commission to humankind was, as noted above, to be fruitful and to fill the earth and to steward it well (Genesis 1:26–31). In the second account of the creation in Genesis 2, there is a similar concept: humans were placed in the Garden, but life flowed from it into the rest of the world. The implication of the text is that our commission is to fill the world with life. Many scholars have noted the indications in the Old Testament that link the whole of creation with the Temple: God's intention was that the whole of the creation should be a place for Him to live.[24]

When God called Abraham — and we do not know why He chose Abraham and his family, but He did — the covenant promise was to bless him and make him a great nation so that "in you all the families of the earth shall be blessed"

---

[24] **N.T. Wight summarises a lot of scholarship on this in an accessible way in** *Simply Christian* **and** *The Day the Revolution Began*

(Genesis 12:3). When the covenant was renewed in Genesis 15, God promised Abraham the land, again as a sign of blessing and fruitfulness, and even His presence with His people. Later in the Old Testament, it became clear the land was given to Abraham's family so that they would be a blessing to the whole world. Just as the Garden is a sign of the blessing to come to the whole world, so was the Promised Land.

The land was promised to God's people, but it remained His possession (Psalm 24:1; Leviticus 25:23). As Michel Sabbah, a former Latin Patriarch of Jerusalem, put it, Israel could only be God's guest.[25] The land was promised with references to borders that are inconsistent in different places in the Old Testament. The land promised in Genesis 15:18 is everything from the Nile to the Euphrates, which is far beyond the territories occupied by David and Solomon, which are in turn far beyond the current geographical boundaries people think of as Israel or Palestine. The literal geography is impossible, but this speaks of an expansion like that of the Garden, to cover all the earth. As Isaiah 2 and Psalm 67 illustrate, the blessings of the land are not to be

---

[25] See Sabbah "Reading the Bible Today in the Land of the Bible"

held by God's people but should become blessings for all people throughout the earth.[26]

The Garden and the land are symbolic pictures, but in the New Testament we see the realities more clearly: the inheritance we have in Christ. Again, that inheritance is not just for our own enjoyment in selfish isolation but for sharing. Another way of looking at this is to see that the Kingdom of God is advancing until all rulers and authorities are brought under Jesus' feet (Psalm 110:1) through our praying and co-operation with the Spirit in supernatural lifestyles and righteous choices. We will see what this might mean in the last chapter.

---

[26] Other references to this include Psalms 2:8 and 72:8,11; Micah 5:4, Zechariah 9:10; Isaiah 54:2–4

31. Purpose: At home forever

Psalm 110 is the part of the Old Testament most often quoted or referred to in the New, and it seems Jesus used it as a key scripture in His explanation of His own role.[27] He has defeated the wicked powers at the Cross (Colossians 1:15–20 and 2:15) and the Kingdom is here. But He must reign in heaven until all things everywhere are under his feet — the Kingdom is coming and is not yet manifested.

Paul gives some insight into what we are doing in this period of overlap between the Kingdom coming and being fully manifested in Ephesians 1. We have been blessed with every spiritual blessing because we are in Christ, and the following verses expand on this. We are chosen in Christ, Ephesians 1:4 states: because we are in Christ, we are part of Him, and He is chosen, so we have the benefits belonging to Christ. In Ephesians 1:10–12, Paul refers to the mystery of God's will which has been made known to us:

> …as a plan for the fullness of time, to gather up all things in him, things in heaven and things on earth. In Christ we have also obtained an inheritance,

---

[27] See Matthew 22:41–46 and the parallel passages Mark 12:36–37 and Luke 20:41–44 for the main teaching, but there are other references, such as Matthew 26:64

having been destined according to the purpose of him who accomplishes all things according to his counsel and will, so that we, who were the first to set our hope on Christ, might live for the praise of his glory.

We have an inheritance in Christ and know this mystery "so that through the church the wisdom of God in its rich variety might now be made known to the rulers and authorities in the heavenly places" (Ephesians 3:10). Paul continues to explain that this purpose "was in accordance with the eternal purpose that he has carried out in Christ Jesus our Lord, in whom we have access to God in boldness and confidence through faith in him" (Ephesians 3:11–12). So, our purpose is to make known God's wisdom to the powers and principalities.

How can we do that? Through "Words, Works and Wonders." By prayer and speaking truth, sharing our lives and our stories, preaching and teaching. By prayer and righteous lifestyles, by action to care for the weak, poor and marginalised and speak up for those who have no voices. By prayer and supernatural signs and wonders.

In Ephesians 2 and the earlier part of Ephesians 3, Paul explains that unity in the church is the single most important thing that demonstrates the wisdom and supernatural activity of God. In New Testament times, the unity between Jewish and Gentile disciples was the key issue. In other ages and places, the diverse groups are usually different, but the principle is the same: unity matters to God because true family relationships are where love is seen, and love matters because it is the essence of God's character. If God can achieve unity in the church, as a result of Jesus' death and resurrection and the responses of all God's people to trust in Him and *remain* or *abide* in Jesus, the powers will not only be legally defeated at the Cross but amazed at the wonder of God's plan being accomplished. That is the purpose of ministries in the church: they are to equip all the saints for works of service (i.e. love) "until all of us come to the unity of the faith and of the knowledge of the Son of God, to maturity, to the measure of the full stature of Christ" (Ephesians 4:13).

Unity and love are what church is all about, and Paul's vision of the completion — when the Kingdom comes in full and is made obvious to all — is summed up in his prayer in Ephesians 3:14–21:

> For this reason I bow my knees before the Father, from whom every family in heaven and on earth takes its name. I pray that, according to the riches of his glory, he may grant that you may be strengthened in your inner being with power through his Spirit, and that Christ may dwell in

your hearts through faith, as you are being rooted and grounded in love. I pray that you may have the power to comprehend, with all the saints, what is the breadth and length and height and depth, and to know the love of Christ that surpasses knowledge, so that you may be filled with all the fullness of God. Now to him who by the power at work within us is able to accomplish abundantly far more than all we can ask or imagine, to him be glory in the church and in Christ Jesus to all generations, for ever and ever. Amen.

When we are strengthened by the Spirit's power and Christ lives in our hearts, we can understand His will and experience or *know* His love which is infinite and beyond knowing. The goal is that we, the people of God, are filled with all the fullness of God. We, together with all God's people, will become a dwelling place or Temple for His presence. The Promised Land and the Garden will encompass the whole earth and "the earth will be filled with the knowledge of the glory of the Lord as the waters cover the sea" (Habakkuk 2:14).

Other pictures of this are the marriage of the Bride, the church, and the heavenly city of Jerusalem, a picture of God's people, coming down from heaven. Heaven and earth will be united and we will be in perfect union and community with Jesus and one another. Revelation 21 brings these two images of Bride and city together. The main characteristic of the new creation is the fulfilment of what the original creation pointed towards but never achieved:

> "See, the home of God is among mortals.
> He will dwell with them;
> they will be his peoples,
> and God himself will be with them…" (Revelation 21:3)

What could be better than that? God will be living with us and we will truly be at home with Him forever.

Appendix

What are the different ways the New Testament describes atonement?

Ransom/Redemption

In Mark 10:45, Jesus said "the Son of Man came not to be served but to serve, and to give his life a ransom for many." The word "ransom" simply means "the price of release" and was most commonly used in New Testament times when purchasing slaves from the slave market. Redemption appears in Acts 20:28 and Titus 2:14. Jesus paid the price of sin for us: 1 Peter 2:24.

The concept becomes distorted and inconsistent with other revelation of God's nature and character if pushed too far. The challenge is identifying to whom the price is paid. Satan? But that gives Satan too much power. God? But that leads to tri-theism (three gods in place of one God in Trinity). The Bible does not explain that but does present us with the idea of ransom or buying back.

Healing/Eternal life

In John 3:14, Jesus refers to the story of Moses lifting up a bronze serpent as a symbolic focus for God's healing of the Israelites. He explains it as a symbolic picture of Jesus Himself being lifted up on a cross, though the significance of "lifted up" was apparently lost on the disciples until after the event. The next verse contains the promise of eternal life for any who believe. So, this brief passage presents the Cross as the basis for two closely linked concepts: *healing* and *eternal life*. And as we saw, Jesus defines eternal life as knowing God in John 17:3.

New covenant

In his account of the Last Supper, Luke emphasises that the prayerful breaking of bread and sharing of the cup among disciples to remember the Cross as instituting a new covenant (Luke 22:20). This signifies a new basis for relationship between God and humans but links to the idea of sacrifice because sacrifices were integral to the Old Covenant.

Sacrifice

The Old Covenant sacrifices were for different purposes: to cover sin, to express thanks and as a sign of friendship with God and within the community. These are types or symbols that are fulfilled in Jesus. The New Testament uses this image in Romans 3:25, Galatians 2:20 and 1 John 2:2.

The key feature of Jesus' sacrifice is that He willingly allowed Himself to be killed and in doing so brought Himself under the wrath and judgement of God. He identified fully with sinful humanity. So, it is not necessary to conceive of Father as needing some payment to buy off His wrath, and Jesus' self-sacrifice demonstrates the loving nature of God (John 3:16). The Father gave and the Son willingly complied at the direction of and by the power of, the Spirit.

There is a range of views around the idea that the penalty for sin had to be paid and that Jesus paid the price in our place. Again, there is a danger of tri-theism or of setting one Person in the Godhead against the others if we push it too far, whereas in fact all three Persons were actively present at the Cross.

Victory

This seems to be the key theme in the gospel presentations in Acts. It is also implied in many of Paul's statements in the epistles, particularly in Colossians 2:13–15. In John 12:31–33 we find it is time for the "ruler of this world" to be judged and defeated, and as a result Jesus will draw all people to Himself. The scope of this cosmic victory is huge. The demonic powers behind the world system are to be exposed, judged and defeated by the Cross.

Paul explains in Colossians 2:13–15 that He triumphed over His enemies in the Cross.

The danger of over-emphasis on this theme, however, is that we miss the nature of God (love) in considering the power of God. We also miss the potential for suffering in this present evil age until the Kingdom comes in fullness.

Revelation of God's love

In Jesus' death and resurrection, we see the nature and character of God revealed: Hebrews 1:1–3 and Colossians 1:15 present Jesus as the visible image (or exact imprint) of the invisible God. The mediaeval monk Abelard developed an approach that has become popular among more liberal theologians: His love evokes a response of love in us. This builds on Jesus' statement in John 12: "When I am lifted up, I will draw all people to Myself." The Cross is seen primarily as a revelation of God's love.

Reconciliation

This appears in parables such as the Good Samaritan and the Shepherd finding lost sheep; it is clearly expressed in Romans 5:11 and Colossians 1:20. Reconciliation appears to be a key theme in the New Testament and a helpful way of understanding the effect of the Cross/resurrection.

Exchange

All sides in the debates about atonement theories accept the significance of this concept or metaphor. The Word (Second Adam) has power to remake the creation because Christ took our place and died for us. We humans experience alienation (the consequence of sin) but He comes to share it. In Romans 5:8 and 2 Corinthians 5:21, there are clear statements that Christ takes our place.

Bibliography

Alan R. Teo, HwaJung Choi, Sarah B. Andrea, Marcia Valenstein, Jason T. Newsom, Steven K. Dobscha and Kara Zivin "Does Mode of Contact with Different Types of Social Relationships Predict Depression in Older Adults? Evidence from a Nationally Representative Survey" *Journal of the American Geriatrics Society*, vol. 63, no. 10, 2015, pp. 2014–2022. https://agsjournals.onlinelibrary.wiley.com /doi/10.1111/jgs.13667

Andrew B. McGowan *Ancient Christian Worship* (Baker Academic 2016)

Benedict *The Rule of Saint Benedict* Chapter 58

C. S. Lewis *The Last Battle* (Lion, 1990) pp. 159–160

Cyprian *De Ecclesiae Catholicae Unitate* (Legare Street Press, 2022) Section 6

Hans Boersma *Heavenly Participation* (Eerdmans, 2011) p. 23

Hans Urs von Balthasar *Prayer* (Ignatius Press, 1986) p. 122

Jürgen Moltmann *The Crucified God: The Cross of Christ as the Foundation and Criticism of Christian Theology* (Fortress, 1993) p. 276

Matthew D. Lieberman *Social: Why Our Brains Are Wired to Connect* (Oxford University Press, 2013)

Michael J Gorman *Abide and Go: Missional Theosis in the Gospel of John* (Wipf and Stock Publishers, 2018) p. xvii. Used by permission of Wipf and Stock Publishers www.wipfandstock.com

Michel Sabbah "Reading the Bible Today in the Land of the Bible" (November 1993) https://lpj.org/storage/2023/12/14/4th-pastoral-letter-of-michel-sabbah-1588926825-pdf.pdf

Thomas A. Smail *The Giving Gift: Holy Spirit in Person* (Darton, Longman & Todd Ltd, 1994) p. 30 & 183

John Wesley *Hymns and Sacred Poems* (1739) Preface

Recommended for further reading

A Church for the Poor — Martin Charlesworth and Natalie Hughes

A Model for Making Disciples: John Wesley's Class Meeting — Michael Henderson

Contagious Disciple Making — David and Paul Watson

Exiles: Living Missionally in a Post-Christian Culture — Michael Frost

Fathering Leaders, Motivating Mission — David Devenish

Global Humility: Attitudes for Mission — Andy McCullough

God Stories — Andrew Wilson

Heaven — Paula Gooder

How to Pray — Pete Greig

Letters to the Church — Francis Chan

Making Disciples: How Did Jesus Do It? — Tony Pullin

Mentoring Matters — Rick Lewis

Microchurches: A Smaller Way — Brian Sanders

One — Steve Clifford

Organic Church: Growing Faith Where Life Happens — Neil Cole

Organic Leadership — Neil Cole

Rouse the Warriors — Steve Uppal

Social Holiness: A Way of Living for God's Nation — Alan Kreider

The Next Christendom: The Coming of Global Christianity — Philip Jenkins

The Spirit-Filled Church —Terry Virgo

Printed in Great Britain
by Amazon

41294161R00116